INTERMEDIATE LOAN

THIS ITEM MAY BE BORROWED FOR

ONE WEEK ONLY

**INTERMEDIATE LOANS ARE IN HEAVY DEMAND,
PLEASE RETURN OR RENEW**

To renew, telephone:
01243 816089 (Bishop Otter)
01243 812099 (Bognor Regis)

Thomas J. Sergiovanni

The Lifeworld of Leadership

Creating Culture, Community, and Personal Meaning in Our Schools

JOSSEY-BASS
A Wiley Imprint
www.josseybass.com

UNIVERSITY OF CHICHESTER

Published by Jossey-Bass
A Wiley Imprint
989 Market Street, San Francisco, CA 94103-1741   www.josseybass.com

Jossey-Bass books and products are available through most bookstores. To contact Jossey-Bass directly call our Customer Care Department within the U.S. at (800) 956-7739, outside the U.S. at (317) 572-3986 or fax (317) 572-4002.

Jossey-Bass also publishes its books in a variety of electronic formats. Some content that appears in print may not be available in electronic books.

The list of recommendations on pp. 33–34 from *Breaking Ranks*, the 1996 report of the National Association of Secondary Principals, is reprinted by permission. For more information concerning NASSP services and/or programs, please call (703) 860-0200.

Figures 7.1 and 7.2 on p. 133, and the statement on Arnold Tannenbaum's theory of power on pp. 134–135, from *Value-Added Leadership: How to Get Extraordinary Performance in Schools* by Thomas J. Sergiovanni, copyright © by Harcourt Brace & Company, are reprinted by permission of the publisher.

Library of Congress Cataloging-in-Publication Data
Sergiovanni, Thomas J.
    The lifeworld of leadership : creating culture, community, and
personal meaning in our schools / Thomas J. Sergiovanni. — 1st ed.
       p. cm. — (The Jossey-Bass education series)
    Includes bibliographical references and index.

    ISBN 0-7879-5028-9 (acid-free paper)
    ISBN 0-7879-7277-0 (paperback)
    1. Educational leadership—United States. 2. School improvement
programs—United States. 3. School environment—United States.
4. Educational accountability—United States. I. Title. II. Series.
LB2806 .S38 2000
371.2'00973—dc21   99-6485

FIRST EDITION
HB Printing   10 9 8 7 6 5 4 3
PB Printing   10 9 8 7 6 5 4 3 2

Contents

The Jossey-Bass Education Series

Preface

Leadership is about many things. At the top of the list is protecting the lifeworlds of our schools. Most citizens want schools to reflect the values and beliefs that are meaningful in their lives. At the heart of a school's individual lifeworld are ideas and commitments that function as a source of authority for what people do. Unlike hierarchical authority or legal authority, authority of the lifeworld influences thought and behavior and provides a basis for deciding things and for authorizing actions based on what people believe about their school and what it is trying to accomplish. This authority exists in the form of local values and purposes and determines local initiatives aimed at achieving the school's own destiny. It will not be possible to improve schools over the long haul if the lifeworlds of schools are ignored and if local authority is short-circuited by heavy-handed mandates from afar.

In this book I explore why the lifeworld of schools is important and show what needs to be done to harness the capacity and spirit of local authority on behalf of school improvement without compromising other legitimate societal interests, such as those of the state. How do we take care of Caesar, in other words, and still maintain the local autonomy each school needs to reflect the values that are meaningful to teachers, students, parents, and others? We will be able to answer this question as we come to understand the importance of institutional character and how it is linked to school effectiveness.

The foundational goal of educational policy, I propose, should be the development and enhancement of institutional character at each individual school site.

Character education is a hot topic these days, as well it should be. As a school improvement theme, character has widespread support from parents and teachers, liberals and conservatives, rich and poor, city and country folk—virtually everyone. In this book I expand the character theme by moving beyond its present focus on individuals, their well-being, their rights and responsibilities, their commitment to the common good, and their willingness to respond to this common good as individuals. I focus instead on character at the institutional level, at the level of the local school. Schools too can be thought of as having or not having character, and institutional character and school improvement go hand in hand.

Institutional character is reflected in the institution's culture. Schools with character have unique cultures. They know who they are and have developed a common understanding of their purposes. They celebrate their uniqueness as a powerful way to achieve their goals. Keys to their success are having control over their own destinies and having distinctive norms and approaches for realizing their goals. Both control and distinctiveness differentiate these schools from schools where character is in short supply. Both control and distinctiveness enhance purpose, identity, sense, and meaning for school participants.

The development of school character and its subsequent effects depends heavily on local autonomy and the wise use of this autonomy. School character cannot develop sufficiently in a decontextualized environment in which all schools look the same and the ideology of "one best way" provides the same standards, curriculum, teaching, and assessment for everyone. A "one best way" may make sense on the assembly line, but what is a good idea in the world of manufacturing is a bad idea in the diverse world of politics and people.

How does leadership fit into this picture? School effectiveness requires authentic leadership, leadership that is sensitive to the

unique values, beliefs, needs, and wishes of local professionals and
citizens who best know the conditions needed for a particular group
of students in a particular context. No "one size fits all" will do.
Leaders with character ground their practice in purposes and ideas
that define the schools they serve as special places and then act with
courage and conviction to advance and defend these ideas.

But creating an effective school involves more than authentic
leadership. It involves instrumental management in the form of good
planning, sound management practices, efficient follow-through,
political sensitivity, and practical engagement skills as well. Authentic leadership and instrumental management are two dimensions that
when carefully balanced support each other. Which dimension represents the fulcrum to this balance is critical; it determines the quality, nature, and expression of the other dimension. Which dimension
is at the center and which dimension is at the periphery, it appears,
is a question of significance in building school character and thus in
predicting school effectiveness.

The German philosopher Jürgen Habermas provides a theoretical
framework and language system for understanding the two dimensions and how they should be balanced. He asserts that all of society's enterprises, from the family to the corporation, possess both a
lifeworld and a systemsworld. In our case, leaders and their purposes,
followers and their needs, and the unique traditions, rituals, and
norms that define a school's culture compose the lifeworld. And the
management designs and protocols, strategic and tactical actions,
policies and procedures, and efficiency and accountability assurances
compose the systemsworld. School character flourishes when the lifeworld is the generative force for determining the systemsworld. And
school character erodes when the systemsworld is the generative
force for determining the lifeworld.

Habermas refers to this latter situation as the "colonization" of
the lifeworld by the systemsworld and attributes many of society's
ills to this situation. In schools, for example, purposes, values, and
beliefs of administrators, teachers, parents, and children are often

decided by state-mandated, standardized assessments rather than the other way around. The result is a loss of character at the individual school site, less authentic leadership, and ultimately less effective schooling.

Habermas's prophecy seems to have come true. The school reform initiatives that took place in the early eighties in the United Kingdom and the United States and that spread rapidly to Canada, New Zealand, and Australia, emphasized national curricula, uniform standards, common reporting requirements, standardized testing, league tables, uniform supervision and evaluation systems, "one best way" models of teaching, and other developments that have removed both uniqueness and discretion from individual school sites. This erosion of the lifeworld places a school's institutional character at risk, endangers opportunities for the exercise of authentic local leadership, and increases the likelihood that schools will be less effective in the long run.

In the United States, loss of character in the public school sector may be the driving force behind the increased popularity of private independent schools, Catholic and other religious schools, charter schools, and other alternative schools. At the moment, these schools seem less affected by reform initiatives that result in the colonization of the lifeworld, enabling them not only to preserve but also to grow their institutional cultures with often dramatic increases in school productivity.

One wonders, however, whether religious schools will still be free to grow their lifeworlds and be faithful to their underlying values as they inch closer to public financial support. Will regulations from the government follow dollars? If so, will these regulations compromise the lifeworlds of these schools? Catholic educators, for example, are fond of quoting from the document *To Teach as Jesus Did* (1973). This document proposes that the gospel message of community and service be the preeminent purpose of Catholic education. Is there an inherent conflict between teaching as Jesus did and the way the state wants?

Many experts attribute the success of religion-affiliated schools not to superior teaching, curriculum, and assessment, and certainly not to bigger budgets and better facilities, but to their ability to generate spiritual and social capital that winds up supporting students' academic performance. Religion-affiliated schools resemble value communities more than they do functional communities (Coleman and Hoffer, 1987; Bryk, Lee, and Holland, 1993).

Will all of this change if discretion is reduced? Will character erode and will the unique lifeworlds of these schools be colonized? Governors and other state officials and corporate executives who support vouchers and other forms of funding for religion-affiliated schools tell us not to worry about these issues. Autonomy will not be compromised. But I believe the public will demand that regulations follow dollars and that ultimately these schools will be held to the same standards, curriculum, teaching, assessment, and other requirements that apply to the public schools. This possibility raises two basic questions. First, will these schools be able to remain unique? And second, if uniqueness is lost, will these schools continue to be effective?

A larger set of questions that are of concern in this book follow. What are the effects of the increased colonization of the lifeworld on school character and authentic leadership? To what extent is character eroding? How are school principals affected by these issues? In what ways is school leadership being redefined? Are some schools more affected by these trends than others? Why is this so? How do parents fit into the picture? How might the standards movement, the push for uniform statewide testing, and other accountability measures be redefined so that they serve rather than determine the lifeworld of schools?

Overview of the Book

In this book I explore these questions while remaining cognizant of two basic principles that have great weight in determining whether schools in the United States and in other places of the world are able to grow their lifeworlds in a way that serves locals well. The power of localism rests upon these two principles as does the future of schooling as a democratic institution. The first is the principle of subsidiarity and the second is the principle of mutuality.

The principle of subsidiarity states that every member of every society and every institution in that society should be free from excessive intervention, circumscription, or regulation by the state or any other larger institution. This principle places faith and responsibility in local rights and initiatives as guardians of the lifeworlds of schools and societies.

The principle of mutuality states that interdependence in the form of mutually beneficial associations characterized by dignity and respect among people, among different institutions, and between different levels of government should characterize relationships. This principle, too, places faith and responsibility in local rights and initiatives as guardians of the lifeworld but sees them as integral parts of a larger community where interests from all levels of this larger community come together on an equal footing.

The bringing together of the principles of subsidiarity and mutuality is one way to build a system of schooling rooted in local lifeworlds but connected to larger societal interests. This book endeavors to show how this goal can be met, how we can craft a schooling system based on layered loyalties and shared accountability that builds on local initiatives and concerns without compromising the legitimate concerns and interests of the state and other stakeholders.

Chapter One examines the role that culture plays in providing a unique framework for each school that allows it to form and grow its lifeworld. Through this lifeworld, connections are formed, relationships are shaped, purposes are discussed, commitments are made, and sense and meaning are experienced by parents, students, teachers, and other locals. This process builds character within the school, increasing its capacity to serve the intellectual, social, cultural, and civic needs of its students. Examples of how this lifeworld is now being eroded in the United States and abroad are provided. The consequences of lifeworld "colonization" on the moral life of local schools and on their effectiveness as teaching and learning institutions are explored.

The problem is framed as one of balance. Should local values, purposes, needs, and requirements that represent the "ends" of schooling determine the more instrumental questions of standards, objectives, curriculum, teaching, and assessment, or should these "means" colonize the lifeworld by being allowed to determine local school values, purposes, needs, and requirements? "The objectives must determine the organization," cautioned the *Cardinal Principles of Secondary Education* (Commission on the Reorganization of Secondary Education, 1918), "or else the organization will determine the objectives."

Chapter Two examines the link between school character, in the form of a thriving lifeworld, and school effectiveness. School effectiveness is broadly defined as a school's ability to achieve higher levels of thoughtfulness among its students, to foster relationships characterized by caring and civility, and to record increases in the quality of student performance on both conventional and alternative assessments. A variety of evidence suggests that schools that function as well-focused communities where unique values are important, where caring for others is the norm, where academic matters count, and where social covenants bring parents, teachers, students, and others into a common commitment get surprisingly good results. Equally clear is that local authority is a necessary ingredient in this school effectiveness equation.

In Chapter Three we explore the virtues that undergird the profession of teaching. These virtues, as combined with the characteristics of effective schools discussed in Chapter Two, are experienced in the hallways and corridors of the day-by-day life at the International School of the Americas (ISA). The ISA story is told in Chapter Three. ISA is a highly successful, nonselective public school of about four hundred students that shares the campus of a larger high school.

Community is the heart of a school's lifeworld. Community protects the school's lifeworld by ensuring that means will serve ends rather than the other way around. Communities require that people come together to share common commitments, ideas, and values and use this core of ideas as the source of authority for what they do. But we live in a diverse society and reaching agreement is often difficult. Can we have community and diversity at the same time? Etzioni (1993) thinks so and asks us to consider the metaphor of a mosaic as a way to think about schools and other institutions that seek to be communities in a diverse society. A mosaic is composed of pieces of different colors and shapes that are held together by a common frame and glue. Can we build schools with this metaphor in mind? Is it possible for us to provide for both diversity and unity in a school by inculcating layered loyalties? These are issues that are examined and illustrated in Chapter Four.

Chapter Five examines the impact of standards and assessments on the lifeworlds of individual schools and local communities. Though the intent may be to design standards and assessments that serve school goals and purposes, too often the standards and assessments wind up determining them. An alternative that relies on layered rather than uniform standards and on shared accountability is proposed. This alternative assumes that it is reasonable for both state and local officials to set standards and craft assessments. States, for example, might set standards for all schools in the skill areas of reading, writing, and basic math. Local schools and school districts might then assume responsibility for setting standards in the remaining areas of the curriculum. This chapter shows how such a system can work to the benefit of all stakeholders.

What we want are good schools. But nailing down just what is a good school is not that easy. Different people want different things. Yet nearly everyone agrees that good schools cannot be defined only by scores on state tests. We rely on standardized testing because we know how to use it and because it is easy to use. In

Chapter Six a broader view of assessment is proposed—one that relies not only on tests but also on other forms of assessment. Further, since the lifeworlds of schools differ and people want different things from schools, in a layered system schools are likely to have different standards that make standardized assessments invalid. To remedy this problem I propose that whole school quality review be adopted. Many other countries have used reviews as part of their "inspection" systems, and this general idea, with modification for our own setting, has merit.

New York state has experimented with the whole school quality review process, and the state of Illinois is now implementing its version of the process. Such reviews, conducted by a visiting team of parents, teachers, administrators, and state officials over a period of several days, examine several dimensions of effectiveness. The basis of the review is a school self-study within which school purposes are delineated, standards are described, and evidence is provided that the school is progressing toward its goals.

In a system of layered standards and shared accountability a review team would base a portion of its assessment on objective standards in basic reading, math, and writing as proposed by the state. The review team would also base its assessments on focused and varied standards in key curriculum areas as developed by the school, and focused and varied standards in social and emotional learning areas as proposed largely by the school. The school's standards in noncurriculur areas, such as the use of resources, school culture and community, and teaching standards, such as professionalism, collegiality, professional growth, and quality of practice, would also be assessed by the review team. Examples of how such a system might work are provided.

Chapter Seven turns to the theme of teachers, their work, and their learning. This chapter is based on a simple premise: the more teachers know and the more skilled they are in teaching, the more successful schools will be in advancing learning. Chapter Seven examines how leadership oriented to the lifeworld can provide the support that teachers need to function more effectively.

In Chapter Eight we turn to the question of change, examining the strategies that support the lifeworlds of schools and bring about changes that affect the quality of teaching and learning that takes place in classrooms. Present change strategies rely on bureaucratic mandates, interpersonal skills and styles of change agents, and market competition, incentives, and individual choice theories. However, professional, cultural, and democratic forces are the means to build professional, covenantal, and democratic community in a school. Alternative change strategies proposed are professional standards of expertise, collegiality, and professional norms; cultural shared values, goals, and ideas about pedagogy and relationships; and democratic social contracts and shared commitments to the common good.

Chapter Nine takes up the question of leadership and its relationship to democracy and the lifeworld. Schools need special leadership because schools themselves are special places. Further, leadership oriented to the lifeworld and to democratic ideals is based on ideas, rather than personality, and the cultivation of a shared followership. For leadership to be effective its moral authority needs to be examined. Leadership, it is argued, addresses normative and spiritual questions and is designed to bring people together in a quest to find meaning and significance in their lives.

Chapter Nine also provides an argument for using *republican* rather than *pluralist* versions of democracy as a framework for understanding how responsibilities should be allocated across the political spectrum from the individual school site to the governor's office. Republican conceptions of democracy, true to the principles of subsidiarity and mutuality, are direct and seek to involve people firsthand in the affairs that affect their personal lives. To make direct democracy work at the local level, certain rules of engagement will have to be provided and followed. The role of the leader in these deliberations is that of generating valid and useful information, helping people to make free and informed choices, and building internal commitment.

Where Do We Go Next?

Respecting differences while maintaining unity is a principle that has deep roots within our constitutional society. Layered loyalties are part of our common experience. Being members of communities that are nested within other communities characterizes our ordinary existence (Etzioni, 1996). Yet these principles seem not to be at the center of our deliberations as school policies are debated and school improvement strategies are initiated. What is lost by this neglect? Democratic ideals essential to preserving and growing the lifeworlds that each of us needs to belong, to find meaning in what we do, to understand how we are connected to a larger and more impersonal world, to express our values and beliefs, and to find significance in our lives. Regardless of what else we do to improve schools, we are not likely to be successful unless these lifeworld conditions are experienced by parents, students, teachers, and others who are locally involved with our schools.

Society places the burden for preserving and growing lifeworlds on its social organizations and institutions. Families, faith communities, mutual benefit organizations, and civic associations are examples. Among social organizations schools have especially important roles to play. Larry Cuban (1998) argues that good schools come in many styles. Some are traditional, others are progressive, and still others are somewhere in between. But regardless of their styles, good schools share three characteristics: parents, teachers, and students are satisfied with them; the schools are successful in achieving their own explicit goals; and graduates of these schools exhibit democratic values, attitudes, and behaviors. In good schools the lifeworld is alive and well.

My intent in writing this book is to identify in practical terms what is at stake for our children, our schools, and our nation as lifeworlds come under increased pressure from often well-intended "one best way" approaches to school improvement. These approaches specify standards, curriculum, organizational patterns, teaching protocols, and assessments that seem now to dominate the school improvement agenda of the United States and many other countries as well. I worry about the numerous contradictions that accompany this movement. Two stand out: the practice of decentralizing *means* to individual schools while at the same time centralizing *ends* at the state level. Over time, the centralization of ends centralizes the very means that are supposed to be decentralized. Meanwhile, there are calls for more choices that will enable parents to select schools and school programs at the same time that schools are beginning to look more and more alike.

We know a lot about what makes a successful school. I summarized some of this knowledge in three other Jossey-Bass books: *Moral Leadership* (1992), *Building Community in Schools* (1994), and *Leadership for the Schoolhouse* (1996). Institutional character is a common characteristic of successful schools. This character has a great deal to do with both schools' academic and social success. School reformers and others interested in improving schools can enhance a school's character by preserving its uniqueness, encouraging the development of a value center that points the way and guides behavior, and providing enough discretion over *both* means and ends so that the school can actually function with character. One thing we know with certainty is that institutional character, like individual character, cannot develop successfully in an environment where discretion has been removed.

The leadership challenge for all of us is formidable. The good news is that, despite a reform climate that often frustrates institutional character, character exists anyway in many places. Further, most people who want to improve schools recognize the importance of individual and collective lifeworlds and their impact on school character. Perhaps this book can make a contribution by focusing attention on these issues and by encouraging conversations that lead to practical strategies for respecting differences while maintaining unity, honoring and using layered loyalties, and viewing schools as communities nested within communities.

In sum, the lifeworld is the essence of hope. The systemsworld is the means to achieve hope. Both are necessary for schools to flourish. Schools and local communities can be the front lines in the defense of hope by maintaining proper balance. Achieving this balance at all levels of government from the statehouse to the schoolhouse may be the most important purpose of leadership.

August 1999   Thomas J. Sergiovanni
San Antonio, Texas

The Author

Thomas J. Sergiovanni is Lillian Radford Professor of Education and Administration at Trinity University, San Antonio, Texas. He received his B.S. degree (1958) in elementary education from the State University of New York, Geneseo; his M.A. degree (1959) in educational administration from Teachers College, Columbia University; and his Ed.D. degree (1966), also in educational administration, from the University of Rochester.

From 1958 to 1964, he was an elementary school teacher and science consultant in New York state and taught in the teacher education program at the State University of New York, Buffalo. In 1966, he began nineteen years on the faculty of educational administration at the University of Illinois, Urbana-Champaign, where he chaired the department for seven years.

At Trinity University, Sergiovanni teaches in the school leadership program and in the five-year teacher education program. He is senior fellow at the Center for Educational Leadership and the founding director of the Trinity Principals' Center. A former associate editor of *Educational Administration Quarterly*, he serves on the editorial boards of the *Journal of Personnel Evaluation in Education*, *Teachers College Record*, and *Catholic Education: A Journal of Inquiry and Practice*. Among his recent books are *Moral Leadership: Getting to the Heart of School Improvement* (1992), *Building Community in Schools* (1994), *The Principalship: A Reflective Practice Perspective* (1995), *Leadership for the Schoolhouse: How Is It Different? Why Is It Important?* (1996), and *Rethinking Leadership* (1999).

1

The Lifeworld at the Center

Most successful school leaders will tell you that getting the culture right and paying attention to how parents, teachers, and students define and experience meaning are two widely accepted rules for creating effective schools. We still have to worry about standards, the curriculum, teacher development, tests, resources, and the creation of appropriate management designs that help get things done. But these concerns will not matter much unless the right culture is in place and unless parents, teachers, and students interact with the school in meaningful ways.

School Culture

Culture is generally thought of as the normative glue that holds a particular school together. With shared visions, values, and beliefs at its heart, culture serves as a compass setting, steering people in a common direction. It provides norms that govern the way people interact with each other. It provides a framework for deciding what does or does not make sense. Culture, Louis (1980) points out, is "a set of common understandings for organizing actions and language and other symbolic vehicles for expressing common understandings" (p. 227).

To be successful at culture building, school leaders need to give attention to the informal, subtle, and symbolic aspects of school life.

Teachers, parents, and students need answers to questions such as these: What is this school about? What is important here? What do we believe in? Why do we function the way we do? How are we unique? How do I and how do others fit into the scheme of things? Answering these questions provides a framework for understanding one's school life, and from this understanding is derived a sense of purpose and enriched meaning. Purpose and meaning are essential in helping a school become an effective learning community—a community of mind and heart. As Thomas B. Greenfield (1973) states, "What many people seem to want from schools is that schools reflect the values that are central and meaningful in their lives. If this view is correct, schools are cultural artifacts that people struggle to shape in their own image. Only in such forms do they have faith in them; only in such forms can they participate comfortably in them" (p. 570).

If you believe as I do that parents, teachers, and students having faith in a school is critical to its success, then this quotation is worth inscribing on the edifice of every schoolhouse. The best indicator of a good school may well be the extent to which its image reflects the needs and desires of its parents, teachers, and students. To be sure, other interests should appropriately be served. But these interests must be conjoined with those of parents, teachers, and students, whose interests must remain important if not central.

Greenfield (1984) maintains that the task of leadership is to create a moral order that binds a leader and others together. James Quinn (1981) puts it this way: "The role of the leader, then, is one of orchestrator and labeler: taking what can be gotten in the way of action and shaping it—generally after the fact—into lasting commitment to a new strategic direction. In short, he makes meaning" (p. 59).

In 1957 Philip Selznick made several points:

> The art of the creative leader is the art of institution building, the reworking of human and technological

materials to fashion an organism that embodies new and enduring values [pp. 152–153]. . . . "To institutionalize" is to *infuse with value* beyond the technical requirements of the task at hand [p. 17]. . . . Whenever individuals become attached to an organization or a way of doing things as persons rather than as technicians, the result is a prizing of the device for its own sake. From the standpoint of the committed person, the organization has changed from an expendable tool into a valued source of personal satisfaction [p. 17].

The institutional leader, then, *is primarily an expert in the promotion and protection of values* (p. 28).

Selznick is pointing to two domains that can exist side by side in a school. One is a technical-instrumental domain and the other is a values domain. One deals with methods and means. The other deals with goals and purposes. When the school places the values domain at the center as the driving force for what goes on and the technical-instrumental domain at the periphery, it becomes transformed from a run-of-the-mill organization to a unique, vibrant, and generally more successful institution. Institutions, Selznick points out, are so important to people and so permeated with values that they become sources of deep meaning and significance and become regarded as ends in themselves.

Organizations, however, are little more than instrumentalities designed to achieve goals—instrumentalities that are constantly at risk. Selznick (1957) notes that organizations are likely to emphasize methods rather than goals, which results in the substitution of means for ends (p. 12). This happens in schools when rules established to help achieve some purpose, tests designed to provide teachers with information, departmentalized structures intended to bring faculty together as communities of practice, and discipline plans implemented to teach students lessons and enhance civility become ends in themselves.

One of the findings revealed in the successful schools literature (for recent examples, see Bryk and Driscoll, 1988; Meier, 1995; and Darling-Hammond, 1997) is that schools that resemble institutions have central zones of values and beliefs that take on sacred characteristics. As repositories of values, these central zones are sources of identity for parents, teachers, and students from which their school lives become meaningful. Meaningfulness leads to an elevated level of commitment to the school, greater effort, tighter connections for everyone, and more intensive academic engagement for students— all of which are virtues in themselves but which have the added value of resulting in heightened levels of student development and increased academic performance.

The Lifeworld

Culture, meaning, and significance are parts of the "lifeworld" of the school. This lifeworld can be contrasted with the "systemsworld." The systemsworld is a world of instrumentalities usually experienced in schools as management systems. These systems are supposed to help schools effectively and efficiently achieve their goals and objectives. This achievement, in turn, ideally strengthens the culture and enhances meaning and significance. When things are working the way they should in a school, the lifeworld and systemsworld engage each other in a symbiotic relationship.

Symbiotic relationships bring together two dissimilar elements in a way that both benefit. Mutuality is key. Mutuality depends upon a level of intimacy between the elements characterized by trust and respect. Mutuality also depends upon parity. When brought together symbiotically the lifeworld and the systemsworld have equally valuable standing.

An important theme in the discussion that follows is that mutuality can only be achieved in schools, families, friendship networks, faith communities, and other civil associations when the lifeworld drives the systemsworld. But when the systemsworld drives the lifeworld, organizational character erodes. In schools this results in many dysfunctions, including high student disengagement and low student performance.

The terms *lifeworld* and *systemsworld,* as general meanings, are borrowed from the German philosopher and sociologist Jürgen Habermas.[1] Habermas uses the language "systemsworld" and "lifeworld" to describe two mutually exclusive yet ideally interdependent domains of all of society's enterprises from the family to the complex formal organization. When contrasted with the lifeworld, the systemsworld, in Habermas's framework, has little to do with "systems theory" and its postulates of interdependencies, systemic change, and the like.

When we talk about the stuff of culture, the essence of values and beliefs, the expression of needs, purposes, and desires of people, and about the sources of deep satisfaction in the form of meaning and significance, we are talking about the lifeworld of schools and of parents, teachers, and students. The lifeworld provides the foundation for the development of social, intellectual, and other forms of human capital that contribute, in turn, to the development of cultural capital, which then further enriches the lifeworld itself. This is a cycle of "cultural reproduction." The systemsworld, by contrast, is a world of instrumentalities, of efficient means designed to achieve ends. The systemsworld provides the foundation for the development of management and of organizational and financial capital that, in turn, contributes to the development of material capital, which further enriches the systemsworld. This is a cycle of "material reproduction." The former is a world of purposes, norms, growth, and development, and the latter is a world of efficiency, outcomes, and productivity.

Both worlds have value. Both worlds are important to the school. And both worlds are important to other kinds of enterprises as well. Let's take the family, for example. Families are concerned with purposes, norms, and traditions; they focus on the protection, growth, and development of their members; and they seek to enhance the meaning and significance that members experience, allowing them to lead a more satisfying life. Families also budget, save for college, plan vacations, have schedules, keep calendars, manage tax records, and worry about operating costs. With proper balancing, the systemsworld and the lifeworld of the family enhance each other. For this relationship to be mutually beneficial in enterprises like families and schools, however, the lifeworld must be generative. It must be the force that drives the systemsworld.

Center and Periphery

In families, schools, and other social organizations there is a center and a periphery. When social organizations are functioning properly the lifeworld occupies the center position. A good way to visualize this relationship is to recall the old adage "form should follow function or function will follow form." When a school makes decisions about means, structures, and policies designed to serve its purposes and values, the lifeworld is at the center. Form follows function. But when school purposes are decided by decisions about school means, purposes, and policies, the lifeworld and systemsworld are no longer properly aligned. Instead the systemsworld dominates the lifeworld. Function follows form.

Let us dig a little deeper into Habermas's theory. Schools grow and maintain their lifeworlds by taking "expressive" and "normative" action. Expressive action is when parents, teachers, and students express their individual needs, visions, values, and beliefs within the cultural context of the school. Normative action occurs when they seek to act in ways that embody the school's shared values, visions, and beliefs.

Schools grow and maintain their systemsworld by taking "teleological" action and "strategic" action. Teleological action involves the setting of objectives and the creating of systems necessary to achieve them. And strategic action involves making appropriate choices among alternative courses of action with the intent of maximizing value. Schools identify purposes, promote visions and values, plan operations, and engage in teaching and learning by embodying all four forms—expressive, normative, teleological, and strategic—of action. Key to Habermas's theory is that all enterprises can be *simultaneously* understood as both systemsworlds and lifeworlds. Equally key is that teleological and strategic actions of the systemsworld should be determined by and should serve the expressive and normative actions of the lifeworld.

Why is it necessary to engage in this lengthy elaboration of Habermas's ideas? Because noting that schools have both a systemsworld and lifeworld and noting that the two worlds must be successfully balanced to function effectively points to a major problem facing schools across the globe. Habermas (1987) refers to this problem as the "colonization of the lifeworld" by the systemsworld (pp. 173, 353–356). Colonization occurs when the systemsworld begins to dominate the lifeworld.

Balancing the two worlds does not deny the fact that one of the two will always be generative. Either the lifeworld determines what the systemsworld will be like or the systemsworld will determine what the lifeworld will be like. Either management systems are uniquely designed to embody and achieve the purposes, values, and beliefs of parents, teachers, and students in a particular school or the purposes, values, and beliefs of parents, teachers, and students will be determined by the chosen (or more likely state- or district-mandated) management systems. Either unique and locally set school visions and standards determine what testing, curriculum content, and teaching styles will be or testing, curriculum content, and teaching styles imposed from the outside will determine local school visions and standards.

Unfortunately, like the proverbial frog sitting in the soon-to-be-boiling pot of water, colonization happens gradually and goes largely unnoticed. As the systemsworld moves to the center, the lifeworld and the systemsworld become separated. This separation is the first step toward colonization. When the systemsworld dominates, school goals, purposes, values, and ideals are imposed on parents, teachers, and students rather than created by them. Further, management systems become ends in themselves, assigning value to schools and students based on adherence to the system's requirements.

Take testing as an example. When the lifeworld dominates, testing reflects local passions, needs, values, and beliefs. Standards can remain rigorous and true but are not presumed to be standardized, universal, or all-encompassing. While tests possess the proper psychometric properties and the integrity of their substance is maintained, the specifics of what is tested reflect local values and preferences. Further, the worth of individuals in schools is not determined by some narrow definition of effectiveness and achievement. Instead, a range of assessments might include not only tests but also students' demonstration of multiple intelligences, performance exhibitions of one sort or another, and other criteria. As the systemsworld dominates, however, what counts is determined more narrowly by bureaucratic mandates, politics, and other outside forces.

Colonization in Rio Vista

The recent closing of the Rio Vista School—a fictional name, as are other names of people and places in this section—in rural Texas provides an example of the tension that often exists between a school's lifeworld and systemsworld and what happens when the lifeworld is colonized by the systemsworld. Rio Vista is nestled next to the Rio Grande River about fifty miles from the town of Sendero, roughly halfway between Big Bend National Park and El Paso (see Stinson, 1995; and Mac Cormack, 1998, for details). Ranch work dominates the economy. Spanish is the first language for most of the children at the school, and many of the roughly forty families who live in Rio Vista maintain close ties with their sister city across the river in Mexico.

The Rio Vista School, part of the Sendero School District, opened about one hundred years ago. It most recently served thirty-eight students on a campus that included a two-room schoolhouse and two trailers. Three certified teachers were employed. The school budget was $173,000 or $4,553 per child. High school students were bussed fifty miles each way to Sendero. In 1995 the Rio Vista School was one of only 254 campuses in the state of Texas that was rated "exemplary." The rating is based on test scores, dropout rates, and attendance. Being one of 254 exemplary campuses placed Rio Vista in the top 4 percent of all elementary schools in Texas.

During the summer of 1998, the Sendero School Board voted 7–1 to close the Rio Vista School and bus its students to Sendero. This decision was made without consulting parents, teachers, or students. The district's superintendent gave several reasons for the closing. Sustaining thirty-eight students and three teachers on a budget of $173,000 was not very cost-effective, and money was tight. Further, there was a critical teacher shortage at the Sendero Elementary School campus, and the reassignment of Rio Vista teachers to Sendero would help enormously with this problem. Moreover, in recent years test scores in Rio Vista had dipped to slightly below the scores of Sendero students. And finally, from a management point of view, it was difficult keeping track of things on a campus that was fifty miles away.

Effective and efficient assignment of staff, wise use of resources, assessing the extent to which students are meeting academic and other standards, and providing supervision are in themselves neither good nor bad. At face value they are legitimate systemsworld concerns that can enhance the growth and development of a school's lifeworld. On the other hand, these same systemsworld concerns can erode or even destroy the lifeworld of a school. The latter seems to be the case in this story. In 1995 Stinson asked Linda Whitworth, a twenty-seven-year veteran teacher at Rio Vista, to explain the school's success in being rated as an exemplary school. Her response was, "We believe in a lot of hard work and we care about our kids. We expect them to be prompt and to do their best work. If they don't, they do it again." She added, "I can't say enough about our parents. They are our ace in the hole. They support us completely and really pull together with the school." Stinson reports that high expectations, hard work, caring discipline, affection, and parental involvement and support were all factors contributing to Rio Vista's success. Clearly small size, sense of community, and the willingness of the faculty to act in loco parentis have to be included on this list. Because of its unique history, its way of operating, its clear focus and commitment, and the high level of support it received from the local community, Rio Vista could be described as a school with character.

Mac Cormack asked long-time Rio Vista resident Lupe Hernandez for her reaction to the school closing. "My father was a student there, and he is ninety now. Some of my brothers and sisters and all eight of my children studied there. It was an excellent school. My children learned a lot, and they were treated very well." What effect does their children having to make a hundred-mile roundtrip have on the views of Rio Vista residents? Felipe Hermosa told Mac Cormack that "There are already some children not going to school. They get too sick, throwing up and all that. They get too nervous. My son wakes up at 1 A.M. screaming that the bus is leaving already. What's going to happen by the end of the year? The kids will be all messed up." Estaban Gonzalez reports that she lets her son Roberto sleep for three hours after coming back from school. Then she wakes him to do his homework and he goes back to sleep. "He's going to get tired and just hate school." She told Mac Cormack that her six-year-old son was no longer going to school. "He vomits before he gets on the bus, and on the bus he vomits twice. So he is staying home with me. For us mothers it is very hard. We have to make our children suffer. How are they going to learn if they come home like this?"

Veteran teacher Linda Whitworth told Mac Cormack that "I'm heartbroken. It's a very traumatic thing to see the disregard [school board members] seem to have for those little bitty kids and their education. It's the end of a one-hundred-year-old tradition."

Mac Cormack says that Whitworth believes the school was closed because of money and politics rather than academics. "They wanted to close that school forever. I don't think we've had an administration that didn't want to close it at least once." Whitworth also maintains that criticism of recent dips in the state test scores ignores Rio Vista's long-term success. Historically, she argues, Rio Vista students have outperformed Sendero students.

From the board's perspective they are acting in the best interests of all the children and not just a few. Ironically, one of the board members told Mac Cormack, "There is no such thing as a bad decision if you have local control." For him local control means a voice for Sendero but not for Rio Vista.

The Rio Vista story is not about good guys or bad guys. Unfortunately, the systemsworld seems to have a life of its own. Means have a way of strengthening and becoming ends in and of themselves. And that seems to be the case here. Despite what they consider to be good intentions, the policy of the board separates the lifeworld and systemsworld and enables the latter to colonize the former. Colonization erodes the character, culture, and sense-making capacity of the Rio Vista school and the people it serves.

Further Examples

Colonization is not just an American but an international problem. Consider several short examples from abroad. Funding in English schools is on a per capita basis, and parents choose the schools they want their children to attend. Thus whether a school has a decent budget or not depends on its ability to attract students. Funding begins with five-year-olds. Yet it is common for many primary schools in England to admit four-year-olds even though no government support is provided for these students. Head teachers reason that accepting four-year-olds provides an incentive for parents to choose a particular school. The children, however, do not always benefit from this arrangement. The payback to the school occurs if these students stay to become fully funded pupils when they turn age five. Jennifer Nias (1995) quotes one embittered primary head teacher as stating, "It's alright for you. When you look at a four-year-old, you see a child. When I look at a four-year-old, I have to see bank notes" (p. 2). Nias believes doing something that one has misgivings about contributes to emotional exhaustion, depersonalization, and other symptoms of burnout among English teachers. Teachers react this way because they feel passionately that the moral-person-related basis for their work is being eroded and replaced by formal accountability and the emphasis on cost-effectiveness.

Recently, I visited a secondary school in New Zealand. This school, built in British colonial style, occupies a beautiful campus and enjoys an excellent academic reputation. Even more beautiful than the school are the brochures it has developed to market itself abroad. They are expensive, glossy, and compelling.

Like the English schools, the schools in New Zealand are funded on a per capita basis and compete with each other for students. They are free, however, to fill empty spaces with students from abroad who pay full tuition.

Empty seats are more likely to be filled by wealthy students from other countries than by poor students with social capital deficits who live in the surrounding neighborhoods. But then again, given the financial constraints that schools face and the costs of maintaining this beautiful campus and its enriched educational programs, seeking tuition-paying students seems like a pretty good idea. The struggle to survive, and indeed flourish, in this particular competitive school context overrides any commitment the school might have to serve all New Zealanders. Not only are less affluent students and students from lower social classes worth less in dollars, they are more difficult to teach and might jeopardize the school's academic standing. This in turn would make further recruitment more difficult. The cycle of material reproduction, in other words, would be interrupted.

Nias (1995) reports similar consequences of lifeworld colonization in England and Wales. She notes that the pressures of competitive testing based on the national curriculum make schools
reluctant to accept homeless people and other difficult students
because they require too much time and resources and are likely to
depress the school's average test scores. Since average test scores are
published and used by many parents as the basis for choosing a
school, the stakes are very high. Without proper resources the
school will not be able to survive. Thus material reproduction
becomes more important than cultural reproduction.

In Scotland, as in many other parts of the world, Catholic and
other religious schools are funded either fully or partially by the government. With funding comes the inevitable systemsworld intru-
sions on the culture and character of the lifeworlds of these schools.
Intrusion typically takes the form of regulations and mandates that
affect everything from building codes to accountability systems and
from curriculum to personnel policies. Consider, for example, the
case of a Catholic high school in Scotland that had some unique
personnel problems but was not free to deal with them in a way that
was consistent with the values the school espoused. Here are the
particulars. A twenty-two-year veteran teacher was abandoned by
her fifty-one-year-old science teacher husband who moved in with
a thirty-year-old language teacher (Savill, 1998). This arrangement
was complicated by the fact that the separated couple's seventeen-
year-old daughter was a pupil at the school. Her mother com-
plained, "It does not make it easy having to see the pair on a daily
basis at work. It causes division with colleagues who have to choose
between me and my husband. . . . The whole staff cannot condone
what my husband is doing to my daughter. All the pupils know
about the affair. It is very hurtful to her" (p. 3).

The official policy of the school board is not to interfere in mar-
ital problems unless the education of students is affected. But given
this school's religious tradition and commitment to teaching certain

moral principles and family values by both word and deed, it would seem that some action, perhaps a transfer of one of the teachers involved to another school, might be advisable. A spokesperson for the Scottish Catholic Church, however, stated that the church was powerless to take any action at all. "Sadly there is nothing that the church can do. Catholic schools in Scotland are totally run, financed, managed by the state. All the Catholic church has is the right of approval of teachers when they are about to receive an appointment." In the United States, there is increased interest in providing public financial support for Catholic and other religious schools. Will regulations that prescribe a one best way in the term of required standards, curriculum, testing, and other policies follow? If they do, will the result be the erosion of character in these schools?

Culture, Community, and Person

Habermas distinguishes three dimensions of the lifeworld: culture, community, and person. *Culture* provides us with knowledge, beliefs, and norms systems from which we derive significance. *Community* lets us know that we are connected to others and are part of a social group that is valuable, and thus we ourselves are valuable. This is a kind of solidarity that ensures that our "individual life histories are in harmony with collective forms of life" (Habermas, 1987, p. 141). Community reminds us of our responsibilities to the common good. As one of my students told me recently, "Culture implies having common beliefs, but community implies working with these common beliefs toward a common good" (Jones, May 1997). *Person* refers to the individual competencies we develop that lead us to reach an understanding of our personal lifeworlds and that help us in our search for individual identity, meaning, and significance.

Erosion of the lifeworld as a result of colonization takes its toll on all three dimensions. As culture wanes in a school, meaning is lost, traditions are ruptured, and parents, teachers, and students are likely to drift in a sea of apathy and indifference. As community wanes in a school, feelings of belonging, of being part of something important, of having a common purpose, are weakened, and parents, teachers, and students experience a lack of connectedness, disorientation, and isolation. Inevitably these developments influence the person. As person wanes in a school, parents, teachers, and students become alienated from themselves, each other, and the school and its work.

The story is often told about the teacher who asked her students, "Which is the greatest problem facing society today, ignorance or apathy?" They replied: "We don't know and we don't care!" In school apathy and ignorance are tightly linked. For students to become the type of "world-class" learners that many politicians and corporate executives want them to be, students have to be connected to the school, to be academically engaged, to be part of a unique and enthusiastic learning community, to be personally motivated, and to want to do well. These learning virtues are difficult to achieve in a school with a deteriorating lifeworld.

"What is the major problem facing schools today?" This was the question asked of students elected to appear in the book *Who's Who Among American High Schools* in 1996. Their worrisome response? Apathy! This is a finding confirmed recently by Laurence Steinberg and his colleagues Bradford Brown and Sanford Dornbusch (1996) in their study of twenty thousand high school students in northern California and Wisconsin. They conclude that curriculum, instructional innovation, changes in school organization, toughening of standards, rethinking teacher preparation, and other reforms will not succeed if students are not engaged—that is, if they do not come to school interested in and committed to learning.

The loss of character in a school that results from an eroding lifeworld forces students to make culture, community, and personal identity for themselves (see Sergiovanni 1992, 1994). Students turn to their own subculture and its norms in search of meaning and significance. Too often the norms of this subculture work against school purposes. Repairing schools and reconnecting youngsters requires that we rebuild culture, community, and person dimensions of the lifeworld of each individual school. Doing so is a way to restore character in a school. If we fail to restore character, then we will fulfill the prophecy of the French philosopher Henri de Saint-Simm: "The government of man will be replaced by the administration of things" (Kaplan, 1997, p. 15).

2

School Character, School Effectiveness

A sk the next five people you meet to list three persons they know, either personally or from history, who they consider to be authentic leaders. Then have them describe these leaders. Chances are your respondents will mention integrity, reliability, moral excellence, a sense of purpose, firmness of conviction, steadiness, and unique qualities of style and substance that differentiate the leaders they choose from others. Key in this list of characteristics is the importance of substance, distinctive qualities, and moral underpinnings. Authentic leaders anchor their practice in ideas, values, and commitments, exhibit distinctive qualities of style and substance, and can be trusted to be morally diligent in advancing the enterprises they lead. Authentic leaders, in other words, display character, and character is the defining characteristic of authentic leadership.

Conger and Kanungo (1987, 1988) propose that leaders are more likely to be viewed as persons of character when they advocate a set of purposes and ideas that are sufficiently unique to challenge the status quo but still close enough to be accepted by followers; when they demonstrate a willingness to take personal risks to achieve their purposes and ideas; when they act in unconventional ways to implement their goals; when they are sensitive to the unique values, beliefs, and needs of followers; and when they rely on ideas, values, and well-thought-out theories to influence others. For Abraham Zaleznik

(1989), character in leadership "is based on a compact that binds those who lead and those who follow into the same moral, intellectual, and emotional commitment" (p. 15). Leaders with character, it seems, ground their practices in unique purposes and ideas and then act with courage and fortitude to advance and defend those ideas. Their practice is authoritative as a result. Character in leadership requires enough autonomy for leaders and for those they represent to actually decide important things. Where there is no autonomy there can be no authentic leadership, and no authentic followership can emerge. Without autonomy, character is lost.

Organizational Character

Character as an individual concept linked to leadership is similar to character as an organizational concept linked to culture. Schools with character, for example, have unique cultures. They know who they are, have developed a common understanding of their purposes, and have faith in their ability to celebrate this uniqueness as a powerful way to achieve their goals. Key to their success is for parents, students, and teachers of each school to have control over their own destinies and to have distinctive norms and approaches for realizing their goals. Both control and distinctiveness differentiate these schools from schools where character is in short supply. Both control and distinctiveness enhance purpose, identity, sense, and meaning for organizational participants.

A school has character when there is consistency between that school's lifeworld and its decisions and actions. This consistency needs to be embodied in the three dimensions of a school's lifeworld discussed in Chapter One and illustrated in Figure 2.1. *Culture* provides the beliefs and norm systems that people need to experience meaning and significance. A school displays character when this culture is consistent with purposes and provides norms that guide behavior. *Community* provides the relationships that people need to be connected, to value others, and to be valued by others. A school displays character when connections take the form of reciprocal responsibilities and when people feel morally obliged to embody these responsibilities in their interactions with others and with the school. *Person* provides the individual competencies people need to develop and understand their own individual lifeworlds. A school displays character when the purposes, hopes, and needs of its individual members are taken seriously by its culture at the same time that these members are committed to the common good.

School character builds when certain virtues are incorporated into its lifeworld. These virtues can be divided into four groups (Fullinwider, 1986): "(1) the moral virtues—honesty, truthfulness, decency, courage, justice; (2) the intellectual virtues—thoughtfulness, strength of mind, curiosity; (3) the communal virtues—neighborliness, charity, self-support, helpfulness, cooperativeness, respect for others; and (4) the political virtues—commitment to the common good, respect for law, responsible participation" (p. 6).

For character to be achieved in a school, that school must enjoy a large measure of freedom. Freedom allows a school to decide what its goals and values are, how the virtues will be expressed given different situations, and the means that will be used to achieve goals and to express virtues.

Figure 2.1. School Character and the Dimensions of the Lifeworld.

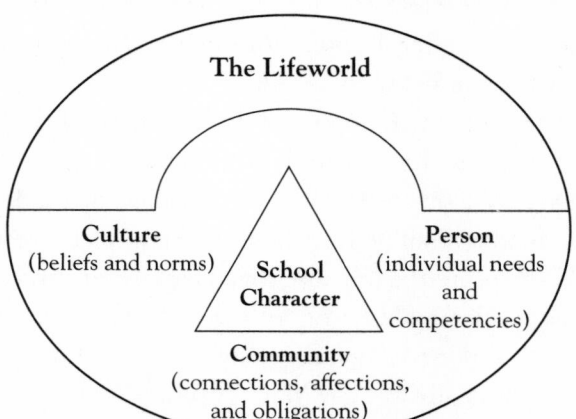

Theories of Schooling

In *Leadership for the Schoolhouse* (1996) I described three theories that have dominated thinking in school administration—the pyramid, railroad, and high-performance theories. Pyramid theory assumes that the way to accomplish school goals is to have one person assume responsibility for providing direction, supervision, and inspection. As the number of people to be supervised increases, management burdens need to be delegated to official managers, and a hierarchical system of management emerges. Pretty soon rules and regulations are developed to ensure that all of the managers think and act in the same way and to provide guidelines for teachers and others, so that they too think and act in the same way.

But most schools and school systems are too complex, and thus it is difficult to control things directly. So then we turn to the railroad theory for help. This theory assumes that you can control the way people think and act indirectly by standardizing the work they do. Instead of relying on direct supervision and hierarchy, the emphasis is on anticipating all of the teaching, learning, curriculum, assessment, and management questions and problems that are likely to come up. Then answers and solutions are developed by higher authorities that represent tracks for all teachers and for all schools to follow to get from one goal or outcome to another. Once the tracks are laid out, teachers and schools are trained to follow the tracks properly, and monitoring systems are set up to ensure that the tracks are followed.

Railroad theory encourages the development of instructional delivery systems in which measurable outcomes are identified and tightly aligned to a set curriculum and to specific methods of teaching. Once instructional delivery systems are in place, teachers are supervised to ensure that the approved curriculum and approved methods of teaching are being followed. Students are tested to ensure that the approved outcomes are achieved. But the railroad theory works clumsily at best. Many teachers and schools do not like being put into straightjackets. Teachers often complain of being "de-skilled," parents sometimes feel they are being left out, policy-makers and administrators worry about bureaucratic bloat, and students find it difficult to be personally engaged in their studies.

New reforms now sweeping across the United States, Canada, the United Kingdom, Australia, New Zealand, and many other countries are based on the high-performance theory. This theory, popularized in such best-selling books as *In Search of Excellence: Lessons from America's Best Run Companies* (Peters and Waterman, 1982), differs from pyramid and railroad theories by de-emphasizing top-down hierarchies and the laying out of tracks that tell people how to do their jobs. Decentralization is key. Teachers and schools are empowered to make their own decisions about how to do things. And parents too are involved. Borrowing from the practices of efficient business organizations, this theory assumes that the way to get control over things is by connecting people to standards rather than by connecting them to bureaucratic rules or to procedural work scripts. Though the standards are a "one best system" of outcomes that applies to all students, teachers, and communities in a particular district, state, province, or country, schools are free to decide how to achieve the standards. Principals, teachers, and parents can organize schools and make decisions about teaching that they think will best enable them to reach the required standards. Data are then collected to determine how well teachers and schools are doing and to encourage them to figure out ways to continuously improve their performance. Statewide standardized student testing is often used to help accomplish this goal.

Means and Ends

What are the problems with these approaches to managing schools? Both pyramid and railroad theories separate the planning of *what* schools will do and *how* they will do it from the actual *doing*. The school district, state, province, or nation is responsible for planning what and how, and principals and teachers are responsible for doing it.

When the high-performance theory is used, schools are provided with standards and then allowed to decide how to achieve them. This is an important improvement over pyramid and railroad theories. But because planning what to do is separated from planning how to do it, one wonders just how different this new theory is.

When means and ends are separated is professional discretion compromised? Are we being true to democratic principles? Are we being sensitive to local school community values, beliefs, and requirements? Since the ends to be achieved influence what means will be used to achieve them, does high-performance theory wind up deciding both means and ends anyway? If we decide that the answer to these questions is yes, then we place at risk the character of individual schools. And since character and performance are linked, school productivity factors are also placed at risk. (I wonder if parents, principals, and teachers are likely to feel empowered by being involved in decision-making processes that are limited to issues of how, but not what—of means but not ends.)

Advocates of high-performance theory in the United States are quick to point out that although state standards are uniform, they have been decided democratically by committees of citizens and experts, including teachers and school administrators. Advocates claim that all stakeholders are represented. I wonder, however, whether this is the kind of democracy that works best in a highly diverse, multicultural society where differences in visions, wishes, and desires of people may be greater within states than between them. When this is the case, giving each state autonomy over the standards it sets does not guarantee local control. Further, even though 80 percent of the people may like a particular standard, the voices of the other 20 percent are too important to be denied—a theme we will pursue further in Chapter Five.

How Schools Improve

What do we know about improving schools? We know that good schools improve one at a time. High-performance theory gets good marks on this dimension by advocating site-based management, local school councils, and other school-based approaches to decision making. We also know that good schools improve on their own terms. High-performance theory is helpful here, too. But does high-performance theory go far enough? Can schools really get better over the long haul by deciding only how they are going to do something that someone else wants them to do? Or, if schools are to improve on their own terms, will families and their schools also have to decide locally such questions as, What is worth doing? What outcomes are valued? What are the standards we believe are important? What standards best match our students' interests and needs?

Good schools are unique. They are unique because they reflect the values of the communities they serve. They reflect the beliefs of the teachers who work in them. They reflect the needs of the students they serve. Why is uniqueness important? Because creating a unique school and being part of a unique school helps us feel special and improves our level of commitment. Shared commitments pull people together and create tighter connections among them and between them and the school. And these factors count in helping students learn at higher levels.

Character and Community

The importance of uniqueness to school character and effectiveness points to a major shortcoming of high-performance theory. If we decide that we really want high-performance schools, then we will have to give more emphasis to bonding. Parents, teachers, students, and their families will need to be bonded together into a "we." This sense of "we" transforms them from a collection of individuals to a collectivity with shared interests. But bonding depends upon everyone being bound to a set of shared purposes, ideas, and ideals that reflect their needs, interests, and beliefs. While being empowered to make decisions about how to implement someone else's policies and goals may help, I am not sure that it is enough to result in the connections needed for schools to work well over the long haul.

The ties that bond and bind teachers, students, and parents together into a moral community are important in the development of a community theory of schools that transcends high-performance theory. As schools become authentic communities they begin to take on unique characteristics. They become defined by their centers—repositories of values, sentiments, and beliefs that connect community members together in special ways. As schools become communities they are less driven by bureaucratic characteristics such as hierarchies, mandates, and rules and by the personalities and interpersonal skills of their leaders. Instead, the school's values and purposes become the driving force. As this happens, a new hierarchy emerges—one that places ideas at the apex and principals, teachers, parents, and students below as members of a shared followership that is committed to serving these ideas.

Community theory places the lifeworld of a school at the center and uses this lifeworld to generate an effective and efficient systemsworld as a means to achieve its lifeworld-defined ends. Pyramid and railroad theories, by contrast, place the systemsworld at the center. This center, in turn, defines and determines the lifeworld of schools. High-performance theory is an improvement by allowing freedom over means. But since the standards and outcomes that schools are to achieve are mandated, it too winds up dominating the lifeworld by determining what will be important, focused upon, talked about, and used to place value on teachers, parents, and students in every school subjected to the mandates. These and other community themes will be discussed further in Chapter Four.

Character and Effectiveness

School effectiveness can be broadly defined as achieving higher levels of pedagogical thoughtfulness, developing relationships characterized by caring and civility, and recording increases in the quality of student performance. The relationship between school character as an organizational concept and this definition of school effectiveness has been well documented (see Hill, Foster, and Gendler, 1990; Bryk and Driscoll, 1988; Sergiovanni, 1994; Meier, 1995; Bryk and others, 1998). Character adds value to a school by contributing to the development of various forms of human capital. Two that are particularly important to this discussion are social and academic capital.

Schools develop social capital by becoming caring communities (see Bryk and Driscoll, 1988; Battistich, Solomon, Watson, and Schaps, 1994; Sergiovanni, 1994). Social capital consists of norms, obligations, and trust that are generated by relationships among people in a community, neighborhood, or society (Coleman, 1988, 1990; Gamoran, 1996).

When students have access to social capital they find the support needed for learning. But when social capital is not available, students generate it for themselves by turning more and more to the student subculture for support. The result, too often, is the development of norms and codes of behavior that work against what schools are trying to do. This seeking of support elsewhere often takes its toll on both academic performance and social behavior.

Uniqueness, discretion, and shared visions derived locally and embodied in norms that guide behavior, consistency, and other life-world concerns are antithetical to schools structured and operated centrally as large complex bureaucracies. Bureaucratic schools are not very effective and efficient developers of social capital. They typically drive students away from connecting to the goals of pedagogical thoughtfulness, academic performance, social and emotional development, and civility. Students turn instead to their own subcultures in search of their own goals and norm systems. As Cusick (1992, p. 6) explains:

> The bureaucracy absorbs students' time, not their energy, and for students in the midst of differentiated and dense routine there is a great deal of waiting around with little to do. Schools mass their people just as do armies,

stadiums, and prisons, where people spend a lot of time
waiting around for others to do something or watching
others do something. In schools, the other is a teacher
who, in the interests of articulating the school's limited
notion of what is appropriate, initiates the activity and
maintains the center of the interaction. Of the mass of
students, schools demand attendance, passive compliance,
and limited attention but not a lot more. Adding up the
time spent on announcements or receiving assignments,
coming and going, eating, waiting, and watching, and
otherwise complying with the procedural demands, students experience a great deal of empty space in the day.

Cusick concludes that "left to themselves, students turn to their
friends, not to their studies" (p. 32). He notes as well that the academic side of the school is much less strongly normed than are peer
groups or the school bureaucracy. However, the norms of the school
bureaucracy, in Cusick's view, are not sufficiently strong to offset the
power of student subcultures. Cusick does point out, though, that
"there is the possibility for students among themselves and for students and teachers to create positive relationships around academic
content" (p. 36). He refers to the work of Grant, for example, as an
antidote to these bureaucratic dysfunctions. Grant (1988), in his
seminal book *The World We Created at Hamilton High*, advocated a
purposive school community as a way to counter peer group norms
and to bring students together as committed members of a learning
community (see also Lightfoot, 1983; Lipsitz, 1984).

Schools develop academic capital by becoming focused communities that cultivate a deep culture of teaching and learning.
The rituals, norms, commitments, and traditions of this culture
become the capital that motivates and supports student learning
and development. Teaching and learning provide the basis for making school decisions. Leaders in focused communities are committed to the principle that "form should follow function," with

function defined by school goals and purposes. They strive to embody this principle as decisions are made about organization, staff, time, money, space, and other resources; curriculum focus, content, implementation, and assessment; teacher development, supervision, and evaluation, and other matters that have an impact on the quality of teaching and learning (Sergiovanni, 1996).

In a focused community there is a strong and clear commitment to academic achievement as evidenced by rigorous academic work, teachers' personal concern for student success, and the expectation that students will work hard, come to class prepared, and complete assignments (see Sebring and Bryk, 1996). This commitment to academic success is more likely to be achieved when the heart of the curriculum is narrowly focused and common for all, assessment is authentic and linked to purposes, standards of achievement are explicit and public, and students are encouraged to do their best.

Teaching and learning in focused communities are characterized by assignments and teaching strategies that encourage students to create knowledge for themselves, to anchor what they learn in frameworks, theories, and disciplinary structures, and to link this learning to real-world problems (Newmann, Secada, and Wehlage, 1995). Schools with a strong and deep culture of teaching and learning know what they are about and communicate this to students in a way that increases their academic engagement and performance.

Academic Press and Community Together

Research on schools that promote achievement points to academic press and community as important factors. *Academic press* refers to strongly communicated expectations that students will work on intellectually challenging tasks, come to class prepared, and complete all assignments (Sebring and Bryk, 1996). One measure of community is personalism. *Personalism* refers to the degree to which students feel personally known and cared for. The two contribute to the development and strengthening of the school's organizational character. As Sebring and Bryk (1996) explain, achieving schools "are safe, orderly, and respectful; they demand that students do significant academic work; and the teachers and staff work hard to provide the students with moral and personal support" (p. 5). Widespread and intense concern for students and support on the part of teachers accompany these themes. Extra help is provided when needed, and students are praised when they try to do well.

In their Chicago research, Sebring and Bryk (1996) found that emphasizing both academic press and personalism had a significantly greater impact on students being academically engaged than did an emphasis on just one factor alone. *Academic engagement,* a prerequisite for student achievement, is defined as the extent to which students are connected to their academic work, try hard, are persistent, and seem committed to learning. These relationships are illustrated in Figure 2.2.

Figure 2.2. Influence of Academic Press and Personalism on Academic Engagement in Elementary Schools.

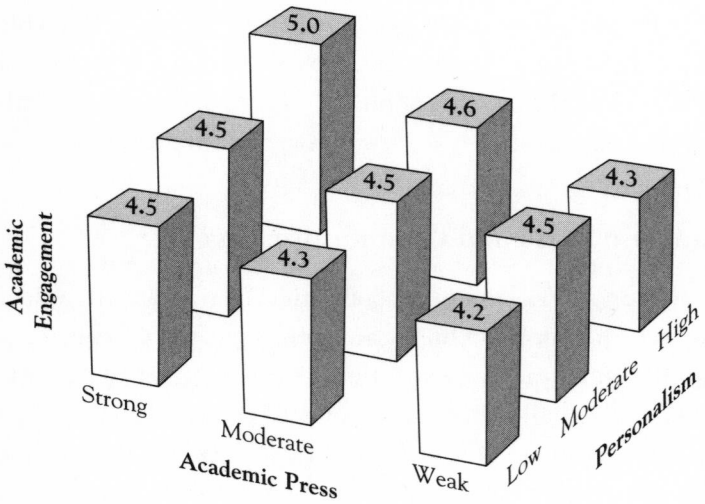

Note: Ratings based on a 0 to 10-point scale.
Source: Sebring and Bryk, 1996, p. 13.

In their seminal study of urban Catholic high schools that were effective with low-income minority students, Bryk, Lee, and Holland (1993) were able to link academic press (high expectations combined with clear and strongly held norms) and a strong sense of community, with increases in academic achievement. Shouse (as reported in Sebring and Bryk, 1996) found that the highest average achievement occurred in schools that provided an emphasis on both academic press and communality. Neither high communality and low academic press nor high academic press and low communality schools were very effective. His study was based on a national sample of high schools serving large numbers of low-income students.

Personalism and academic press together are important in helping schools become interdependent, caring, and focused communities able to generate increased levels of civility and academic performance. But neither caring nor academic performance can be scripted. Both must emerge from the school's sense of what is important, the school's inventory of values and purposes, the school's commitment to do well, and other lifeworld concerns that provide a school with character.

Character in Focused Schools

The RAND report (Hill, Foster, and Gendler, 1990) provides further evidence of the link between school character and school effectiveness. This report was based on an analysis of thirteen high schools in New York City and Washington, D.C. Some of these high schools were Catholic, others were public comprehensive schools, and still others were public special-mission or magnet schools. The research found that the more successful schools in this sample (the Catholic schools and the public schools with special missions) had unique, clear, and simple purposes centered around improving student academic performance and attitudes and providing the care, concern, and organizational arrangements necessary to help students achieve their goals. The Catholic and public schools with unique and clear missions were labeled "focus schools," and their more undifferentiated and less effective public school counterparts were labeled "zoned schools." In the words of Hill, Foster, and Gendler:

> Focus schools [both Catholic and public] resemble one another, and differ from zoned comprehensive public schools, in two basic ways. First, focus schools have clear, uncomplicated missions centered on the experiences the school intends to provide its students and on the ways it intends to influence its students' performance, attitudes, and behavior. Second, focus schools are strong organizations with the capacity to initiate action in pursuit of their missions, to sustain themselves over time, to solve their own problems, and to manage their external relationships. . . . [S]tudents and staff in each focus school consider their school special, a unique creation that reflects their efforts and meets their needs [p. vii].

Hill, Foster, and Gendler contrast these different schools as follows: "Zoned public schools, in contrast, have diffuse missions defined by the demands of external funders and regulators. They are also profoundly compromised organizations, with little capacity to initiate their own solutions to problems, define their internal character, or manage their relationships with external audiences. Because zoned schools are essentially franchises reflecting a standard model established by central authorities, staff and students have less reason to consider the schools uniquely their own" (p. vii). Not only did focus schools concentrate on student outcomes but they also established social covenants that communicated reciprocal responsibilities of parents, students, teachers, and administrators. Further, they had a strong commitment to caring and rallied around a set of values and ideas aimed at increasing levels of caring and civility as well as academic performance. Their curriculum was limited, allowing for concentration on what was considered important. And perhaps most important, *focus schools had discretion*. They were relatively unencumbered by central office, state, and other bureaucratic mandates. In short, focus schools were able to grow their lifeworlds and to use their lifeworlds as the generative force and the source of authority for what they did. Focus schools had systemsworlds, too. But the purpose of the systemsworld was to serve the schools' ends, not shape them.

Hill, Foster, and Gendler, for example, point out that focus schools are built around themes of uniqueness and specialness. They have specific educational and ethical principles (central zones) that are used to guide behavior. (The characteristics of focus schools identified by Hill, Foster, and Gendler are summarized in Exhibit 2.1.) The authors point out that to preserve uniqueness and to keep the moral center of these schools strong, staff members need to be deeply involved in and invested in constructing strategic and tactical purposes and operations. Since focus schools are unique, they provide real alternatives to parents, teachers, and students—alternatives from which to choose. Zoned schools, by contrast, are much more undifferentiated. It is assumed that one size fits all, and thus these schools do not provide authentic alternatives from which teachers, parents, and students might choose.

Breaking Ranks

With the publication of *Breaking Ranks: Changing an American Institution* in 1996, the National Association of Secondary School Principals (NASSP) joined the struggle to strengthen the lifeworlds of U.S. high schools. The word *struggle* is deliberate because of strong pressure from many reformers to replace our traditional "one best way" of doing things with a cleverly designed, yet unobtrusive, new version of "one best way" in the form of uniform standards for everyone. When the same standards for all areas are imposed on everyone in a state or a country, they become the driving force for everything important that local schools do. As a result the lifeworlds of

Exhibit 2.1. Characteristics of Focus Schools.

Common Elements

- They are organizations with definite missions and cultures, not simply chance aggregations of individuals who happen to be assigned to the same work site.

- Their distinct characters set them apart, in the minds of their staff, students, and parents, from other schools. Though not all focus schools have unique or highly innovative curricula, each has a special identity that inspires a sense of loyalty and common commitment.

- They are committed to education in its broadest sense—the development of whole students. They induce values, influence attitudes, and integrate diverse sources of knowledge. They also transmit facts and input skills, but mainly they try to mold teenagers into responsible, productive adults.

Common Attributes

- Their clear and simple missions focus on students.

- They operate under an internal social contract that motivates discipline and academic effort.

- They are committed to parenting and to teaching practical ethics as a central part of their educational responsibility.

- Their curricula are designed to draw all students into a common core of skills and intellectual experiences.

- They consider themselves problem-solving, not program-administering, organizations.

- They work self-consciously to sustain their own capabilities and organizational character through the selection and aggressive socialization of new faculty members.

- They are accountable to the people who depend on their performance rather than to central rule-making, auditing, or assessment organizations.

Source: Adapted from Hill, Foster, and Gendler, 1990, pp. 55–56. Reprinted by permission.

parents, teachers, and students at each individual site are likely to be compromised.

Breaking Ranks proposes a number of important lifeworld-oriented reforms, including emphasizing teacher capacity building, developing small (no larger than six hundred) idea-based learning communities within schools, providing each student with an adult advocate, not allowing teachers to see more than ninety students per term, and requiring that teachers and administrators prepare personal learning plans. Listed next are four of the eight recommendations from *Breaking Ranks* that relate specifically to curriculum (1996, p. 11):

1. *Each high school community will identify a set of essential learnings—above all, in literature and language, mathematics, social studies, science, and the arts—in which students must demonstrate achievement in order to graduate.*

If the identification of the most essential learnings takes place at the local level by parents, teachers, and students in each school, then the lifeworld will be preserved. If, however, all of these learnings are mandated, and if all of the specifics of what students must demonstrate to graduate are also mandated, then the lifeworld of the school will be threatened.

2. *Teachers will design work for students that is of high enough quality to engage them, cause them to persist, and when successfully completed, will result in their satisfaction and the acquisition of skills and abilities valued by society.*

Implicit in this recommendation is that teachers will be able to decide a major proportion of what this work will be. This discretion is essential not only to preserve the lifeworld but also to provide the right situational context for teachers to teach well and for individual learning needs of students to be met.

3. Assessment of student learning will align itself with the curriculum so that students' progress is measured by what is taught.

This recommendation is key. Assessment is a desirable tool that can provide both those in the school and the general public with important information about how well students are learning. A good assessment system, however, is a shared one with individuals at each local school site playing important roles.

4. Each student will have a Personal Plan for Progress to ensure that the high school takes individual needs into consideration and to allow students, within reasonable parameters, to design their own methods for learning in an effort to meet high standards.

This too is a key lifeworld recommendation that depends upon a strong commitment to local school autonomy for success.

So close, yet so far. *Breaking Ranks* points directly to organizational character as an important quality for leveraging change. If *Breaking Ranks* seeks to create a new generation of high schools, virtually all of its recommendations will require a high degree of localism for them to be translated into sensible practices. Parents, teachers, and students together with their principals will have to decide for themselves the kinds of schools they want to create to get the kind of commitment needed to create them. A viable, growing, and efficacious lifeworld is essential to do this. The kinds of changes that *Breaking Ranks* is talking about will require the abandoning of a tradition—a tradition of "one best way." At the same time, such changes will require that schools adopt a new view of accountability—a shared view; a new view of democracy—a layered view; and, indeed, a new view of community—a diverse view. These are the themes that will be addressed in the next several chapters. But first let's turn to Chapter Three for an example of how one school, the International School of the Americas, is struggling to build character and to become more community-like in today's diverse society.

3

Competence and Caring in Action

To many, teaching is a profession founded on methods of teaching and mastery of the disciplines to be taught. Though both these components are important, even necessary, neither is sufficient to define teaching as a profession. To teach is to profess something, and professing requires standing for certain virtues that include making a public commitment to serve ideas and people. Caring is the cornerstone of this commitment. Noddings (1992), for example, believes that schools should be defined as centers of care and that themes of caring should permeate every aspect of school life from relationships and organization to curriculum and teaching. Caring, according to Beck (1994), involves promoting human development and responding to human needs. This idea equates teaching with caring and caring with teaching as one and the same activity. Both depend on the cultivation of special kinds of relationships among and between teachers and students that are characterized by a measure of reciprocal commitment. As James Comer often says, "In the real estate business it is location, location, location. In education it is relationships, relationships, relationships."

The Virtues

Mayeroff (1971 as cited in Beck, 1994, p. 10) refers to the needed commitment as "devotion" that is demonstrated by "being 'there' for the other in a way that is the converse of holding back and ambivalence. Viewed over an extended period, it is shown by . . . consistency, which expresses itself as persistence under unfavorable conditions and in . . . willingness to overcome difficulties." Devotion may be too strong a word for impersonal professions that deal with things but not for caring professions. William Arrowsmith (1985) captures the essence of teaching as follows: "I spoke earlier of this teaching as an activity resembling love. There is in it, or should be, a sense of compassion and care; a care for the species, for what it might be, for the young, for their fulfillment. Insofar as teaching is a profession, it is one [that] was founded not on a body of methods or disciplines, but upon service, on an inspiriting ethos of presumably efficient love. In theory, at least, teaching is unselfish" (p. 56).

These thoughts of caring and serving as foundational anchors for defining the profession of teaching are reminiscent of van Manen's (1991) emphasis on pedagogy as leading children in such a way as to provide direction for their lives. He states, "whether we like it or not every pedagogical action is normative: It shows how one is oriented to children and how one lives up (or fails to live up) to one's responsibilities" (p. 35). Following Aristotle, van Manen sees pedagogy as a "good" or a "virtue" that every teacher and parent must practice. He defines pedagogy as an "encounter of togetherness between parent and child, teacher and pupil, grandmother and grandchild—in short, a relationship of practical action between an adult and a young person who is on the way to adulthood" (p. 31). Like love and friendship, he continues, "pedagogy is cemented deep in the nature of the relationship between adults and children" (p. 31). Following van Manen, we can speak of three lifeworld conditions of pedagogy: loving care for the child; hope for the child; and responsibility for the child—all of which provide a moral basis for the practice of teaching. These conditions are at the center, driving the more instrumental systemsworld conditions needed to make schools academically, socially, and developmentally effective places for all of our students.

The International School of the Americas (ISA)

Service to people and ideas and caring are professional virtues that contribute to and provide the substance for a school's character. In this chapter these virtues are illustrated by examining life in the hallways and classrooms of the International School of the Americas (ISA), a small school in San Antonio, Texas. This school has a vibrant lifeworld filled with purpose and meaning that operates like a compass by providing direction. At the same time, ISA has an effective and efficient systemsworld that operates like a well-thought-out road map that helps the school identify and achieve its goals and purposes. As a result, ISA enjoys a high measure of academic success while at the same time being a model community characterized by caring.

For several months during the 1993–94 school year, my colleague John Moore and I invited seven people representing Valero Energy Corporation, Southwestern Bell Corporation, and Trinity University to join us in a conversation that led to the founding of the school. Chula Boyle, who was then on loan to Trinity University from her school district and serving as director of Trinity's Principals' Center, was involved in this conversation. Boyle later became the founding principal of the school.

What were the nine of us up to? We wanted to help willing teachers, parents, and students create a school with character—a school that would stretch the way that most of us in San Antonio were then thinking about such issues as school size, curriculum, teaching and learning, collegiality among faculty, roles of students and parents, and student discipline and assessment. We were influenced by what experts were saying about creating sensible high schools and paid particular attention to the Coalition of Essential Schools ideas. We were also very conscious of what was going on at Central Park East Secondary School in New York City and at other successful schools that were making headlines.

Our strategy was to propose design principles that an interested group of educators could use to create their own school. The school we hoped to create had to be unique; levels of ownership in the school among parents, teachers, and students needed to be high; and the lifeworld of the school needed to be the central and generative force for what the school would do and how it would operate. We were, therefore, not interested in developing a model of organization, curriculum, teaching, and assessment that would merely be imported by a school.

These are the principles that were proposed to provide the basis for planning the school. They were offered as talking points that would be refined in practice.

- We believe that a diploma should reflect that a student has mastered a number of essential skills and is competent in certain areas of knowledge.

- We believe that the curriculum should be simply organized, with a few important goals providing compass settings for learning. The emphasis should be on mastery of what is essential.

- We believe that focusing on the basics of learning provides a start for lifelong learning.

- We believe that students learn best in settings characterized by intimacy and caring.

- We believe that the needs of young people are the driving force for the choices they make. Particularly important are the following needs:

  The need for mastery, to be challenged, and to accomplish important things

  The need to belong, to be accepted without condition

  The need for autonomy, to take risks in a protected environment, to try new things, to spread one's wings

The need to care, to cooperate with others, and to feel needed as a result

- We believe that providing for these needs should be of prime concern in developing school policies as they relate to teaching, curriculum, scheduling, discipline, counseling, athletics, the school's social climate, and other concerns.

- We believe that emphasis should be on the work that needs to be accomplished and the learning desired rather than on the clock or the calendar.

- We believe that the school should be organized and operated in a way that enables students to learn how to become active citizens and caring adults, to know and care about our community and world, to know and care about themselves and others, and to demonstrate this caring.

- We believe that learning should be organized around the mastery of learning exhibitions. Exhibitions should be supplemented, when appropriate, by traditional courses in areas such as foreign language, physical education, advanced mathematics, and other areas.

- We believe that students should be viewed as active learners who will accept responsibility for their own learning by meeting together, planning their work, arranging their schedules, monitoring their progress, and being responsible for providing teachers and others with compelling evidence that they are learning.

- We believe that simplicity should be emphasized in making curriculum decisions.

- We believe that cooperation and teamwork should be emphasized, and teaching and learning should be organized in ways that encourage or require students to work together, to help each other, to solve problems.

- We believe that the school should be small and should take advantage of its size by calling on students and teachers to assume a greater share of responsibility for running the school.

- We believe that students should complete a community-oriented service project as part of the requirements for graduation.

When Richard Middleton, superintendent for the North East Independent School District in the greater San Antonio area, learned about the opportunity to create a new school, he proposed that it be in his district. Lee High School was chosen as a site for the school and five teachers along with Boyle stepped forward to help make this school a reality. They began by examining the general principles and where they stood on these and similar issues. This led to the framing of a set of operational principles and values that provided the basis for designing a curriculum, a pattern of organization, and a policy structure for the school.

The Voices of Teachers

In the section that follows vignettes prepared by ISA teachers Heidi Anderson, Nikki Lopez, and Liz Moore and by the school's first principal, Chula Boyle, are provided. They are reflections on the early years of the school (Anderson, Boyle, Lopez, and Moore, 1997).

The International School of the Americas opened its doors to 113 freshmen in the fall of 1994 with five teachers, one staff person, and a director, creating the first magnet school in North East Independent School District in San Antonio, Texas. Creating this school was risky because, in this part of the country, most magnet schools build in success by "selecting" their students. ISA guarantees that all children who make the choice to apply will have equal opportunity to be drawn from the lottery for enrollment. In the end, the group reflects the demographics of San Antonio and North East Independent School District high schools. Students who have never passed a class in middle school to students who were at the top of their eighth-grade classes fill ISA's halls. And they all come for the same reason. They want something different, they want a smaller school, they believe in the power of their own choice.

We began with hope, desire, and a lot of promise to bring ISA students a quality learning experience that would guarantee each and every one of them access to post-secondary education. What did we promise? We promised students small classes, caring teachers, the right to have a voice in their learning and in their futures, and the ability to learn in ways that would mix traditional with non-traditional approaches. We told them there would be no tracking. We believed everyone was gifted. There were no modern classrooms, very few computers, borrowed materials, and a stripped-to-the-cement-floor former vocational education lab that served as home. The challenge was to bring reality to the idea that choice, regardless of a student's learning history, could invigorate and excite learning within the child. And, it would happen in an environment that guaranteed support and care during their learning.

Consider, for example, Rosa, a student at ISA. Rosa called to tell us how things were going for her in her senior year. She waxed eloquent about her love of English as a class, how smart she feels as a writer, how she understands and loves to talk about great literature. She told me about a conversation she had been in with six other seniors. Rosa had led the conversation about *Hamlet* and Shakespeare as a writer. She led the conversation while she and the others were sitting away from the rest "catching up" on their work. This particular group still struggles with being students. Traditional assignments hold little appeal to them. Yet there they were completing the hated assignments and talking about *Hamlet.*

What kind of leadership invites students to recognize themselves as powerful learners? What kind of leadership helps them to understand the learning game? Learning is, in school anyway, about showing other people what you know. What kind of leadership invites students to know the power that lies within themselves? At ISA we define leadership as voice and care and support with dashes of hope and expectation. This kind of formula is not just for the Rosas of the world, but for any person who walks into ISA's community. Teachers, staff, parents, students, mentors, business partners—everyone is expected to be a leader and everyone is expected to have a voice. True leaders stir up, guide, and nurture the characteristics of leadership in others no matter how faint or deeply embedded. Some of our students come to ISA timid and fretful, but we recognize and rejoice in their gifts and encourage them to speak up and to speak out.

Carlos, during his freshman exit portfolio interview, reminded us of how much our school presses students to develop their power and potential. He said, "Miss, when I first walked through the doors of ISA, I walked with my head down like this." He demonstrated a tentative walk, head down, eyes cast to the floor, an exact replica of the shy, soft-spoken boy I knew a year ago. "But now, I walk like this!" Carlos's stride was confident, with his head held high and a wide smile brightening his face. He looked us straight in the eye, proud of his growth. The transformation stunned me. Here was a young man, eager to tell his story, to give his opinion, and thought-fully to question the status quo. We had succeeded.

Leadership is different here at ISA because teachers and students work together to make decisions that ulti-mately impact the students and their learning. Doing what is best for students guides our every decision. That is why ISA children are always a part of the interview process for new teachers. ISA has never had a teacher who did not fit when the kids were involved with inter-viewing. We show kids right away that each one of them has a voice, and we challenge them to use it! Voice requires being heard and being listened to and having the ability to hear and listen. Voice requires patience and understanding. It requires seeing as many sides as possi-ble, and it allows for many different opinions. It causes us to know enough about what we want or believe in to convince others. It also demands the ability to be con-vinced. Having a voice means being open, honest, and extraordinarily flexible. Voice can be noisy and chaotic. It can look like confusion. It requires thinking about yourself while thinking about others. Of course, it takes time and patience to develop productive, supportive, thoughtful voices. But within a very short amount of time, our students rise to the occasion.

In our first year of existence, students formed the Stu-dent Advisory, a diverse group that represents the voice of the students in the dialogues. Membership is not selec-tive but rather is a voluntary commitment to attend meetings and participate in Board activities. The original Advisory took responsibility for articulating and writing the Code of Ethics by which all ISA community mem-bers agree to abide. In our second year, the Advisory re-examined the Code in an attempt to define its ideas more concretely. Though this dialogue took almost a year, and though we hit several points where our frustration level grew intense, the Advisory discovered the wide variety of personal experiences that govern the concept of respect. In the end, the students decided that the best way to explain the Code was by using the Golden Rule: "Do unto others as you would have them do unto you." Once they arrived at this conclusion, the Advisory members designed a workshop on the Code that they presented to the entire school population. Passing on the ideas behind and embedded in this Code has become a tradition for the Advisory Board as we add each new class. Those students who were involved in this process have become real leaders of dialogue in the Advisory, as well as in other areas of the school and larger community. Carol, one of the original members of the Board, said, "It is up to those of us who have been here the longest to pass our experiences on to those who are coming behind us . . . to teach them what we discovered so that they can pass along the ISA way to those that come behind them."

Incorporating such a wide variety of leadership abilities and styles into the foundation of a school takes an immense amount of trust. When we ask students for their feedback on a project or the curriculum of a class, we trust that they will take this job seriously. And actually, it has never crossed our minds that they would behave any differently.

At a school assembly, a tapping foot, the liquid sounds of a saxophone—and then a pause fills the room; a six-foot student dressed as Aretha Franklin turns his head toward the crowd. Students smile and laughter roars as the show continues to the tune of "Respect." The next morning, school items that had disappeared . . . returned, no questions asked. ISA's success has always lived within its students. It is an expectation. When students teach students the values of life, such as respect, a bond of friendship is formed and a ripple is created that touches the future.

Classroom Life

Kathy Bieser and Jennifer Baize (1998) studied the classroom lives of teachers and students at ISA, relying on interviews, classroom observations, and their own experiences as interns at the school. They found that classrooms at ISA could be characterized as crowded, alive, relaxed, loud, informal, and open. Students feel that they are the school and that they own and make the school. They found classrooms to be student-centered and students to have a strong voice in their own learning. To them "the most critical factor in defining the classroom culture at ISA is the teacher-student relationship. At ISA the relationship between teacher and student is friendly, open, relaxed, and caring. One ISA student explained she could ask an ISA teacher anything about the school or her personal life and the teacher would respond openly. It is easy to ask for help and receive it from teachers during class" (p. 2).

In studying the student-to-student relationships in classrooms Bieser and Baize concluded that cooperation and teamwork were valued components in the classroom. The type of work that students were assigned and did provided excellent examples of this high level of cooperation. "The majority of assessments at ISA center around group-oriented, interdisciplinary projects. Projects motivate students to spend time doing their work and to stress quality over quantity. There is less emphasis on daily drill and homework. Class discussions are an important part of the learning that takes place in the classroom and are highly valued by both teachers and students. . . . Student work fills the classrooms and halls at ISA. Work from all types of learners is displayed. Desks and tables are arranged in groups to facilitate discussion" (pp. 3–4). In sum these investigators found that the basic classroom culture at ISA placed a great deal of emphasis on teacher-student relationships that were family-like and group-oriented and that maximized student voice. These characteristics were based on the assumption that open relationships between teachers and students resulted in greater academic, social, and emotional growth; that group work is not only beneficial to students during their school years but is a long-term investment in their future development; and that student voice is vital to student growth and achievement.

Graduation Requirements

ISA seniors complete a senior portfolio and an exhibition as part of their graduation requirements. The specifications for these requirements are provided in Exhibit 3.1. The senior portfolio is designed for students to answer the question, "Who am I as a learner?" Each portfolio includes a collection of writing in six areas: self, community and school, academics, language and technology, internships, and plans for the future. Five minutes of the student's explaining and defending of his or her portfolio must be conducted in a foreign language. The portfolio and accompanying exhibitions are examined by the student's advisor, senior class teachers, a "significant adult" evaluator, and a peer evaluator. The entire senior class assembles as an audience for each student's exhibition.

Students also engage in an internship that requires 120 hours of documented work in up to three placements. Written documentation in the form of an Internship Folio includes a history of the enterprise, business, organization, or project for which the student worked; a description of the student initiative; reflections on what was learned from the internship experience; a write-up from the internship mentor; and logs and other important artifacts. Here are some of the responses of the students to the question, "What did or will your internship involve?"

Exhibit 3.1. The ISA Senior Portfolio and Exhibition.

Definition:

The senior portfolio is your answer to the question, "Who am I as a learner?" It is a collection of written documents and other artifacts that are presented before several evaluators and an audience of your peers at a formal exhibition. The portfolio represents the culmination of your years at ISA and is a requirement for graduation.

Purpose:

The purpose of the portfolio and exhibition is to provide all ISA seniors with the means to articulate themselves as learners, culminating and synthesizing the experiences and learning that comprise their years at ISA. It will be a unique, individual, public exhibit of each ISA senior's fulfillment of the ISA graduate profile.

Evaluation:

Several people will evaluate your portfolio at your exhibition. They will include your advisor, a significant adult from outside of school, another ISA senior, and your senior teachers. The evaluation will be conducted using the Senior Portfolio and Exhibition Rubric.

Advising:

Your advisory teacher will serve as your advisor for your portfolio, monitoring your progress, checking your work, giving you feedback, and determining your grades. If you wish, you may ask an additional subject area specialist from school or the community to advise you on your particular theme as you develop your portfolio and exhibition.

The Portfolio:

The portfolio is something to take with you when you leave ISA. It should represent you—your skills, your talents, your visions. It should demonstrate who you are, your ideas, and your goals. The portfolio must be a physical object but might take a variety of forms such as a binder, a computer disk, a piece of artwork, an audio cassette, or a video cassette to name some examples.

The Written Component:

Each portfolio must include or be accompanied by a collection of writings that address your educational development in each of six specific areas: self, community and school, academics, language and technology, internship, and plans for the future. A written reflection (minimum 450 words, typed) on each area is required as part of your completed portfolio. The internship reflection corresponds to the written reflection required as part of your Internship Folio that will be included as part of your Senior Portfolio.

(continued)

Exhibit 3.1. The ISA Senior Portfolio and Exhibition, cont'd.

Foreign Language Component:

Five minutes of your exhibition must be presented in a foreign language. This portion must be written out and checked by a foreign language teacher ahead of time. You are encouraged to avoid reading your presentation, but are allowed to read the foreign language component if needed.

The Exhibition:

The portfolio exhibition will be scheduled for the week before fall semester exams and the week before spring break. Each exhibition will last 15–20 minutes. All portfolio exhibitions must be completed by March 12, 1999. The Senior Team will arrange for your advisor and senior teachers to be present at your scheduled exhibition time. You will arrange for your significant adult evaluator and peer evaluator to attend. You are also encouraged to invite your internship mentor(s) and others who have given you guidance and support. The ISA senior classes will come together as an audience for the exhibitions. All exhibitions will be videotaped.

Source: International School of the Americas, 1998.

- I wrote, directed, and edited the recruiting video for our school.

- I will be an International Internship Ambassador in Mexico through an organization within the Mexican government known as Community Promotions, learning administrative and financial systems as well as participating in bringing basic services to rural communities.

- I observed surgery, placed a cast on a foot of a staff member, and assisted doctors in other medical procedures.

- I worked in the pediatric clinic where I took vital signs, observed doctors, measured, weighed, and did head circumference measurements for well-baby checkups.

- I am monitoring the Valero [Energy Corporation] computer network throughout Texas.

- [I am] creating a web page that highlights all of Valero's community involvement.

- I observed and assisted in liposuction, laser-surgery, and hair transplant procedures.

- I audited the company's procurement cards and cash advancements.

- I assisted the San Antonio Spurs staff before and during the games by organizing and setting up the on-court promotions.

- [I] work with my former math teachers to assist them in eighth-grade math classes, and [I] tutor small groups of students.

- I researched information and assisted in show preparations for a live radio talk show.

- I was granted my own project of helping grow cells for the study of osteoporosis and cancer.

- I found the ratio of nonexempt assets to the unpaid debts for a client. I also researched a closed court case to determine how to handle it after the statute of limitations for an appeal expired.

- I will develop the Model United Nations Project for ISA in conjunction with the World Affairs Council.

- I taught a Spanish-speaking girl to read English.

How do ISA students stack up academically? Judging by the accomplishments of its first graduating class in the spring of 1998, very well. Ninety percent of the ninety-two students graduated with an advanced diploma. Ninety-three percent were college bound. Seventeen percent were the first to graduate from high school in their family. There were five National Merit Commended Scholars, three Hispanic Scholars, and six Advanced Placement Scholars. ISA had the largest percentage of students in the North East School

District taking the PSAT and the SAT and their scores exceeded both the state and district averages on verbal and mathematics subtests.

The Voices of Students

Recently, Christer Blomqvist, a Swedish secondary school principal, interviewed three ISA students, Marie, Carol, and John, ISA teachers Liz and Kelly, and Shari Albright, who is in her second year as principal of ISA. Blomqvist was interested in how the culture of ISA was perceived by students and teachers and what unique values and beliefs influenced the school's culture. An annotated and abridged version of his interview follows:

PRINCIPAL: What makes the school special?

MARIE: The teachers are great. They get involved in what you do, in your personal life, your school life and your social life. They support you, and they really see you. They're there for us twenty-four hours a day if we want them.

CAROL: I definitely agree. The teachers are wonderful. I've been at the school since it began. And the commitment of that first team of teachers—they were there from seven in the morning till seven at night almost every day. They had so much commitment. Another of the major assets of the school is the family-type environment. Especially in the first class I was in. Everyone knew everything about everyone. There were no secrets. The teachers, because it is such a small school, they knew each of the students individually. They knew what it would take for each student to succeed. They made the adjustments in their classes. They worked individually with the students. They catered to their different learning styles.

MARIE: In most schools you say, "The principal, oh my God, the principal!" Here the principal is always open, and she is always out there with you, gives you a hug, and encourages you. We students have programs, like clubs, so we have a lot of freedom, a lot of choices.

PRINCIPAL: Do teachers work extra hours at ISA and is this a source of controversy?

KELLY: We operate in a teaming environment. Each grade level is teamed. You work in a team with five other teachers. It really gives you the opportunity to have discussions about kids and about what they're doing in every class. I think that is one of our biggest assets.

SHARI: We have made a big point over the hiring of teachers. We do work extra hours. And actually it isn't the right place for everybody. Some people have left because teaming wasn't right for them. But, for the most part, since there is so much support from other people that are either on your team or are members of the staff, it's really worked out for most people. We also have an understanding that maybe I can stay today, but I have another commitment tomorrow. But that doesn't mean that I'm not pulling my load.

LIZ: On Wednesdays the staff stays after normal school time to give extra lessons and computer lessons. They also give Saturday school. They just are there offering kids who need extra time help. Many come because they really need it. Some come just because they want to hang around school on their Saturday morning.

SHARI: When I leave school at seven o'clock in the evening I actually have to tell kids to go home. They feel it's their school and that it's a good place to be. That's the formal thing about it. The informal thing is that we have teachers who take students almost every week to the symphonies. We have tickets donated to us. We have teachers who meet students there. Or students say to a teacher, "I would love to go to some jazz" and they go to . . . for an early show, when it isn't too smoky. For us who take students there it's an experience. We meet groups of students at a museum on Tuesday night when it's free admission. Those are not things that we say at school that you must do.

PRINCIPAL: What about the relations among the students? Do the Hispanic students stay together?

ALL STUDENTS: No, no, no!

MARIE: In our freshman year we learn, without even knowing that we learn it . . . we do these projects where they mix you with different people. They put you with someone from another school, from the other side of town. It's hard in the beginning because you're not used to that person and his way of thinking is different and he shows what you can do academically in a different way, and we just learn slowly, especially in our freshman year, to be with different kinds of people.

CAROL: Miss Moore [Liz] is laughing because she knows that in my freshman year I was exceedingly frustrated. I was tracked into a gifted and talented class throughout my elementary and middle school years. We moved quickly through everything. And then I came to ISA, and I was with people who had learning problems or didn't catch on quite that quickly, didn't move on that fast, and I was so frustrated. But like Marie said, they paired me with people who were really different from me. Quite honestly I didn't particularly like that the first year. I was very unhappy that they did this to me. At first I tried to force them, saying "Come on, move with me." Then I started settling down, learning from them, and realizing, just because they don't move quite so quickly or just because they don't understand the same things and think differently, that doesn't make them any less of a person. I really got to know other people that otherwise I would never have met. And by our senior year we were all working together. As a class. It was interesting to see things like the portfolios and other projects we were working with in our senior year. You saw seniors choosing other people from the class who weren't particularly their friends, but they knew that they were their complement, that they could put through the other half of the project that they themselves couldn't have done. We knew each other's strengths and we knew each other's weaknesses and we knew how to work together. Much because of things we were forced to do and didn't like during our freshman year. And it was really interesting to watch that development during four years and to watch our class change and grow together.

PRINCIPAL: And you don't think you have learned less because you've worked with people who worked slower than you?

CAROL: I would say I probably have learned a lot more. People who grow up in a socially and economically challenged area, people from the south side, have an entirely different perspective on just about everything from people who grow up in a rich neighborhood. You get exposed to those different perspectives, and you get to hear people's points of view, and you go, "That sounds pretty cool." Even in classes where there aren't many points of view, like in math—I was always very strong in math—I've become a better mathematics student because my friends who aren't so good in math come to me, and I have to reteach them something that I have just learned. That makes me a stronger student. I think it's an asset to me, as well as for anyone else, that they stick everyone together.

PRINCIPAL: What are your academic results compared to other high schools in Texas?

SHARI: Let us compare us with other high schools within our school district, which is a high-ranking school district within the state of Texas. We're second only to the highest socioeconomic status high school. We believe that we're doing highly academic things with our students that are untraditional. You don't see our students sitting in rows very often doing book and paper and pencil work. Our students are very involved. They're very active. They are working with one another. They are doing what we hope is more real-world type work. Even our mathematics classes—there are five projects—final examinations took place in an amusement park. Students took the mathematical functions of Algebra Two and looked for examples in the rides and had to calculate different mathematical functions, which they saw in physical structures. I was floored by the work produced by our students. Their ability to calculate curve and rate of the increase of a downhill. . . . All these things were remarkable to me. And I think these kids walked away with such an amazing grasp of what Algebra Two really means. Those are the kind of things that we're striving to do.

Can a school be a caring place, a place where students are academically engaged, a place where standards are high and learning is rigorous, and a place where high levels of civility are evidenced—all at the same time?

The evidence summarized in this chapter suggests that the answer to these questions is yes, if a school's character is alive and well. Successful schools are focused schools with a strong sense of purpose and a unique way of doing things. This brief look at ISA gives us an idea of what character can look like in the everyday life of a school. Character counts most when it is reflected in a school's teaching and learning, a theme of the next section.

Character in Teaching

It is generally recognized that learning is a process of active construction of meaning; learning is a social phenomenon that best takes place within the context of a learning community; learning is situated in a specific context with different contexts leading to different learning consequences; and differences in learning are a resource (see Wilson and Peterson, 1997). Learners need to make sense of what they are learning and thus interpret and understand what is being taught in terms of their own personal experiences, prior learnings, values, and beliefs. This process of interpretation and understanding is influenced by the interactions a learner has with other learners and by the norms that emerge within a learning group. Some learners will respond to learning something in one context but are not able to learn the same thing in another context.

Take, for example, youngsters who are learning math on the street by running a baseball pool that has meaning to them and that involves a "street level" learning community. If such youngsters are placed at a desk to work alone in a typical classroom, the same math will go unlearned. These students are able to pass the math test of life but fail the standardized test of school. And finally, since learners come to their learning with different backgrounds, capacities, interests, and understandings, they benefit from interacting with other students and learning from other students.

Responding to what we know about learning requires that schools be able to make unique decisions that match their purposes and match the needs and interests of their students. And unique decisions require discretion not only at the school but also for teachers in each of the school classrooms. Both uniqueness and discretion, as we see at ISA, build school character. Consider ISA student Carol, for example. She reported being tracked into gifted and talented classrooms during her elementary and middle school years. At ISA she found herself in the middle of a real-world mix of student backgrounds, talents, interests, and abilities. When asked if she had learned less because she was working with this broad mix of students her reply was, "I would say I learned a lot more." ISA has had the freedom to choose not to track with good results.

One of the principles of the Coalition of Essential Schools is that teachers have to know students well in order to teach them well. For this to happen teachers must focus not only on the methods of teaching and the mastery of their disciplines but also on making a commitment to serve and to care. On this theme the principal Shari Albright comments, "I don't think I've been part of a faculty that is more student-centered in my life. The first thing these teachers ask when they come into the team is not 'What is good for my teaching?' but 'Is this the right thing for this individual student?' It is a very different perspective on secondary education. It is a very individualized and personalized perspective" (Blomqvist, 1998, p. 7).

Judith Deiro (1997; see also Deiro, 1996) tells the story of a teacher and her junior high school students who were returning from a schoolwide assembly on sexual and personal harassment issues. Four college students presented short vignettes depicting harassment ranging from poking fun at how someone was dressed to teasing a female by snapping her bra strap. Once the class was settled the teacher asked:

> "How many thought the assembly was realistic?" Dead silence. No one ventures a response. "My stomach got tight during the vignettes," she says. "They brought up memories of painful experiences for me." She continues, "How many of us have been hurt by harassment or have hurt others?" A few students slightly wave their hands or quietly nod their heads. Pam [the teacher] then tells a vivid story about how, when she was in the seventh grade, she ridiculed a neighbor girl in an effort to gain the approval of a certain group of kids. She discloses how embarrassed and ashamed she still feels about the incident even to this day. A couple of students begin to talk. They share their own stories, talking about times when they harassed someone or when they were harassed. They talk about how they could do things differently. Many students join in. They talk about the possible reasons human beings are so mean to each other. They question the difference between flirting and sexual harassment. They discuss what they could realistically do if they were sexually harassed and caught up in peer pressure in harassing someone else [p. 193].

The teacher, Deiro notes, used *self-disclosure* as a strategy for evoking discussion on the issue and keeping the discussion focused, candid, and honest. Self-disclosure was one of six strategies Deiro identified that the six teachers she studied used to bond with their students. This strategy, along with that of creating one-to-one time with students, were the two used most often by nearly all the teachers. Other strategies included having high expectations of students while conveying a belief in their capabilities; networking with parents, family members, and friends of students; using rituals and traditions within the classroom; and building a sense of community among students within the classroom.

All six of the strategies were used regularly by teachers at ISA. This is because with the lifeworld intact, character and professionalism are intertwined. In schools with character, teachers make it a point to maintain and grow high levels of competence, and they also make it a point to pay attention to caring and community building. Professionalism is about both. Competence alone is not enough. For a true profession to emerge, competence and caring need to be joined together into a seamless practice of teaching. This definition of professionalism is essential in helping schools become learning communities in a diverse society—the theme of Chapter Four.

4

Community in a Diverse Society

Community is at the heart of a school's lifeworld. It provides the substance for finding and making meaning and the framework for culture building. Think of community as a powerful antioxidant that can protect the school's lifeworld, ensuring that means will serve ends rather than determine them. Communities are collections of people who come together because they share common commitments, ideas, and values (Sergiovanni, 1994). Schools can be understood as

- Learning communities where students and other members of the school community are committed to thinking, growing, and inquiring and where learning is an attitude as well as an activity, a way of life as well as a process

- Collegial communities where members are connected to each other for mutual benefit and to pursue common goals by a sense of felt interdependence and mutual obligation

- Caring communities where members make a total commitment to each other and where the characteristics that define their relationships are moral in character

- Inclusive communities where economic, religious, cultural, ethnic, family, and other differences are brought together into a mutually respectful whole

- Inquiring communities where principals and teachers commit themselves to a spirit of collective inquiry as they reflect on their practice and search for solutions to the problems they face

Three characteristics are important in gauging the extent to which a school forms a community: the extent to which members share common interpersonal bonds, the extent to which members share an identity with a common place (for example, my class, my space, my school), and the extent to which members share a commitment to values, norms, and beliefs. Community strengthens connections. As connections in the school strengthen, webs of obligation are created that have moral overtones. The school begins to speak to members in a moral voice. Soon this voice compels them to respond to community purposes and norms (Etzioni, 1993).

What is the story of community?[2] How does this story differ from other stories about schools? What narrative does the story of community encompass? What stories compete with community for the attention of policymakers and administrators in education? The story of community includes unique ways of thinking about connections. In most schools connections are understood using the narrative of *social contracts*. In schools that are becoming learning and caring communities, connections are understood using the narrative of *social covenants*.

The major story line in the narrative of social contracts involves a deal. Each of the parties to the contract gives up something to the other party to get something else back. In this narrative, teachers, parents, and others invest their talents and energy in the school and its children in exchange for certain benefits. Similarly, children endure the rituals of schooling to get the gold stars and praise they covet from teachers, the attention they want from their parents, and the grades they need to be admitted to college. This social contract with the school is maintained as long as each of the parties gets what it wants. When teachers no longer receive the contracted benefits, they are less willing to invest in the school. And when students no longer get the benefits they seek, they are less willing to endure the rituals of schooling. This narrative is about calculations involving trades that offer incentives in exchange for compliance. Self-interest is presumed to be paramount, and "let's make a deal" is the order of the day.

The narrative of social contracts guides the practice of the principal of Locke Elementary School. He promised the student body that if two thousand books were read during the month of October, on Halloween night he would dress up like a witch and kiss a pig on the school building roof. This goal was achieved, and to the apparent delight of the students, the deed was done. The Locke principal believes that contracts are important motivational devices. He reasons that unless teachers, parents, and students get something tangible for their efforts, they will not be motivated. You can't expect a manager to manage well, a worker to be diligent, or a football player to play hard unless there is something in it for them. So, he asks, how can we expect teachers to teach well, parents to parent well, students to learn well, and schools to improve themselves without incentives? How can we expect, for example, teachers and students to display proper behaviors without providing exhaustive lists of rules and regulations or outcome requirements that are linked to clear consequences for noncompliance?

Social Covenants

The major story line in the narrative of social covenants is much less conditional. In this narrative connections are more moral than calculated. Marriages, extended families, civic associations, faith communities, caring groups, and friendship networks are examples of affiliations characterized by covenantal relationships. In the narrative of social covenants, connections among people are created when they are together connected to shared ideas and values. Once achieved, this bonding of people and this binding to ideas forms a fabric of reciprocal roles, duties, and obligations that are internalized by group members. This is a fabric that cannot easily be torn apart when a person no longer likes the deal—a fabric that perseveres even when the fun is gone, when needs are not being met, and when self-interest must be sacrificed.

The narrative of social covenants guides the practice of the principal of Rousseau Elementary School. She encourages teachers and students to work together to develop a framework of values and norms that inform how everyone in the school should lead their lives together. Connected to a larger vision of school purposes, critical values, and pedagogical beliefs, this "covenant" provides the basis for an ongoing discussion about how teachers, administrators, parents, and students can meet their commitments to each other and to the school. Students at Rousseau, for example, expect teachers to work hard, to be caring, and to teach well. Since relationships are reciprocal, teachers expect students to respond similarly. Students are given considerable latitude in deciding important things at Rousseau. They help decide how learning goals will be achieved and help make decisions about how they will spend their time. But decisions must be responsible ones that embody and enhance the school's covenant. Both teachers and students work hard to make reading fun and useful while also increasing mastery. Rousseau's students are avid readers as a result.

The Rousseau principal believes that when given the opportunity to make important decisions about school goals, purposes, and values, teachers and students will respond by morally embodying these goals, purposes, and values in their actions. Further, the bonding of school members together and their binding to shared ideas and ideals provides a normative environment that encourages moral responsiveness. Social contracts, she reasons, have important roles to play in the real world. But so do social covenants. The school is the place, she argues, to learn about social covenants, to practice developing them, and to use them in a practical way to govern affairs.

In comparing the two narratives, Sacks (1997) argues that a social contract is maintained by the promise of gain or the threat of external force. A social covenant is maintained by loyalty, fidelity, kinship, sense of identity, obligation, duty, responsibility, and reciprocity. A social contract, he points out, is instrumental, serving important political and corporate ends that ideally are in the national interest. A social covenant, by contrast, is concerned with quite different institutions—families, communities, friendship groups, and voluntary associations are examples. Social covenants provide the basis for our civil society. A healthy civil society also serves the national interest by being the moral foundation, bedrock, and wellspring that provides cultural purposes, unity, and strength. Social contracts are at the core of what connects people in formal organizations, and social covenants are at the core of what connects people in social organizations. The former are rule-based and the latter are norm-based.

Building Community in Schools

In the story of school as community, connections, relationships, and commitments are governed more by social covenants than social contracts, and schools function as social organizations that are distinct from formal organizations.

I was in Rochester, New York, recently and had a chance to walk through the downtown area. Being a Xerox Corporation fan, I decided to visit the beautiful Xerox Tower that graces several plazas close by. Xerox is arguably one of the world's best-run corporations, and many of its views about leadership and other management themes have been exported to other organizations with good results. Inside the main corporate foyer are huge portraits of Xerox's former chief executive officers (CEOs), each with memorable quotations designed to inform and inspire. I was particularly taken with the portrait and remarks of Joseph C. Wilson who was CEO from 1961 to 1967.

This is what Wilson's inscription said: "In the long run, our customers are going to determine whether we have a job or not. Their attitude toward us is going to be the factor determining our success. Every Xerox person must resolve that their most important duty is to our customer." This is good advice, but is it universal advice? I don't think so. Though his thoughts make sense for Xerox and for other corporations, one wonders about its fit for schools. What Wilson is talking about is a social contract whose terms are simple: serve the customer and you will have a job. Serve the customer well and you will have a good job. Fail to serve the customer and you will not have a job. But what happens when jobs are not at stake? Does that mean we need not worry about commitments to serve others well? Serving the customer, it appears, has little to do with caring for them unconditionally or with other altruistic purposes. Rather, serving the customer is an effective and efficient way to serve one's self-interest. When self-interest is no longer at stake, customers run the risk of being abandoned.

Certainly Wilson offers good advice for people who work at Xerox. But I feel a bit uncomfortable if this is supposed to be the way we do things in the family, in the church, in the volunteer organization, and in the school. In schools, for example, we should pay attention to our students, parents, and others because it is right to do so. It is good, just, and decent to do so. We should pay attention to our students because we have a responsibility to act in loco parentis, and we have a moral obligation to function as stewards on behalf of their parents and on behalf of the schools we serve. Winning a race may be okay for Coke and Pepsi, but somehow this sort of thinking seems strange when applied to family settings, to children, to our spiritual ties, and to other social aspects of our lives.

Despite good intentions, applying customer thinking to the wrong kind of enterprise has unanticipated negative consequences.

For example, when parents and students become accustomed to being considered customers by a school, the demands they place on the school are not only likely to increase but also to focus on their own private needs and self-interests. This selfish customer mentality erodes commitment to the common good and neglects the cultivation of collective responsibility for that good. What is best for all of the students and for the school become secondary considerations.

A few blocks away from the Xerox Tower, I bumped into Rochester's new Bausch & Lomb library building, and inscribed on its edifice were these thoughts: "Progress of the world depends almost entirely on education." "We believe that what ought to be done can be done." "We now turn our hearts and minds to our enlightened teachers." The older Rundell Memorial Library building across the street proudly wore these inscriptions: "Social science: tools forged in altruism to achieve human betterment; embodiment of man's vision of social justice." "Literature: the storehouse of knowledge of the record of civilization; the fulcrum for the lever of progress." "Education is more than preparation for life[;] it is life itself." What a contrast to the messages found in the hallowed halls of Xerox. Xerox speaks the language of social contracts and the library speaks the language of social covenants. Both languages are true. Both languages are necessary. But only one of these languages makes sense for schools as communities.

Communities are organized around relationships and ideas. They create social structures that bind people to a set of shared values and ideas. Communities are defined by centers of values, sentiments, and beliefs that provide the needed conditions for creating a sense of "we" from the "I" of each individual.

In schools that are becoming communities, connections are based on commitments, not trades. Teachers and students are expected to do a good job not so that they can get rewards but because it is important to do so. Discipline policies are norm-based, not just rule-based as in ordinary schools. Instead of relying primarily on trading rewards and punishments for the right behavior, learning communities seek to connect members to what is right and wrong, to obligations and commitments, and to moral agreements. When these moral connections are in place, students and teachers are compelled to action by obligations to embody shared commitments and values. In schools that are becoming communities, members live their lives with others who have similar intentions. In ordinary schools, by contrast, relationships are constructed by others and become codified into a system of hierarchies, roles, and role expectations.

Building Blocks for the Learning Community

Becoming a learning community involves the cultivation of certain building blocks that provide a different framework for what we do, why we do it, and how we do it (see, for example, Sergiovanni, 1994). To be a learning community a school must also be a

- Community of relationships

- Community of place

- Community of mind and heart

- Community of memory

- Community of practice

As the school becomes a community of relationships, connections among people are close and informal, individual circumstances count, acceptance is unconditional, emotions are legitimated, sacrificing one's self-interest for the community is common, relationships are intrinsically valued, knowledge is valued and learned, and students are accepted and loved. These kinds of relationships among people create a unity that is similar to that found in families and other close-knit collections of people.

As a school becomes a community of place, connections among people are strengthened by sharing a common location. The sharing of place with others for sustained periods supports connections by providing the continuity needed for creating a shared identity, a shared sense of belonging, and a shared commitment to caring. Nell Noddings (1992) believes that for community relationships to build, there must be continuity in purpose and that the first purpose is caring for each other. Noddings also believes that there must be continuity in school residence, which enables students to stay together in one place long enough to acquire a sense of belonging, and there must be continuity of teachers and students who stay together singly or in teams for three or more years.

When teachers, students, and parents are connected to the same ideas, connections to each other are further strengthened. A community of mind and heart emerges from this binding of people to common goals, shared values, and shared conceptions of being and doing. Becoming a community of relationships, of place, and of mind involves the development of webs of meaning that tie people together by creating a special sense of belonging and a strong sense of identity.

Community understandings have enduring qualities. They are taught to new members, celebrated in customs and rituals, and embodied as standards that govern life in the community. Further, they are resilient enough to survive the passage of members through the community over time. As suggested by Bellah and his colleagues (1985), enduring understandings create a community of memory. In time communities of relationship, of place, and of mind become communities of memory that provide members with enduring images of school, learning, and life. Community of memory sustains parents, teachers, and students when times are tough, connects them when they are not physically present, and provides them with a history for creating sense and meaning. The substance of a school's community of memory is often enshrined in its symbols, traditions, rites, and rituals.

A community of practice is perhaps the defining benchmark for identifying how deep community is in a school. In ordinary schools, teachers are involved in their own private practices. A school of thirty teachers is defined as a collection of thirty individual practices. In the learning community, individual practices are not abandoned but are connected to shared practices. At the school level a single practice of teaching exists that is shared by everyone. Within this single practice several smaller communities of practice emerge as groups of teachers band together around common themes. As a sense of shared practice develops, collegiality functions at a higher level than is normally the case.

Problems with Community

Community theory is not without its problems. Although community is designed to bring people together for altruistic reasons, community may create systems of "blood" that divide people (see Sergiovanni, 1992). The hard reality is that community, like fire, can be helpful or harmful. By its very nature, community is both inclusive and exclusive. It can bring some people together while leaving others out. Further, community can exaggerate differences with others, causing fragmentation, disengagement, and conflict.

These are serious issues because the world is a diverse place. Diversity raises important questions for how community should be understood, particularly as a construct for schooling. How, for example, do we reconcile the seemingly paradoxical problem of creating distinct school communities that are held together by common meanings and a shared sense of the common good within a society that is increasingly multicultural and that has a strong history of individualism? In schools, how do we identify a common purpose, develop a coherent practice, rally parents, teachers, students, and administrators to common themes, and construct a framework of shared norms when people have different expectations, when teachers have different pedagogical philosophies and work styles, and when the potential for conflict is high?

Many voices suggest that in a postmodern world the very definition of community must be changed. Furman (1998), for example, claims that definitions of community based on unifying concepts and ideals are at odds with the purposes and practicalities of multiculturalism, and by implication, she denies the possibility that a productive moral leadership can emerge from such concepts and ideals. Furman proposes a postmodernist conception of community: "Postmodern community is community of difference. It is based on the ethics of acceptance of others with respect, justice, and appreciation and on peaceful cooperation within difference. It is inspired by the metaphor of an interconnected, interdependent web of persons engaged in global community" (p. 312). But, I would argue, even this definition has a unifying center. Acceptance of others and cooperation within differences are the universal values postmodernists claim are needed to guarantee feelings of belonging, trust, and safety essential to building community. These postmodernist "core values" place a high priority on building a community of relationships as a central part of a school's community of heart and mind.

One problem that contributes to worries about creating stifling communities with rigid centers that divide and exclude people is the perception that centers and sameness are the same. Communities of relationships, heart, and mind need not and should not be built upon all-encompassing, narrowly defined, carbon copy norms but on norms of caring and collaboration. Collaborative cultures share common beliefs in the value of both the individual and the group (Nias, Southworth, and Yeomans, 1989). Such norms as praise, appreciation, help, support, encouragement, and the viewing of differences as learning opportunities are common in collaborative cultures.

As Jennifer Nias (1995) points out, collaborative cultures "should not be mistakenly viewed as conflict-free or cosy. Collaborative cultures are also built upon a belief in the value of openness, tempered by a respect for individual and collective security" (p. 9).

Nothing in the social sciences or in moral philosophy prohibits a community from holding the view that differences can be assets and should be respected.

Amitai Etzioni (1995), relying on his analysis of Charles Taylor's work (1995), offers "principled decentralization" as an antidote to possible divisions among different communities. Within a framework of principled decentralization, localized communities encourage a variety of different voices and interests, not as isolated entities, but within a larger coalition built around common goals and ideas and bounded by a framework of mutual respect. Etzioni (1996, 1997) offers the *mosaic* as an image of community with bounded autonomy. A mosaic is composed of elements of different shapes and colors that are held together by frame and glue. The mosaic symbolizes a society in which various communities maintain their cultural particulars while recognizing that they are integral parts of a more encompassing whole. Within this image, communities have firm commitments to both their uniqueness and their shared framework. And community members have layered loyalties in the form of allegiance to two different dimensions of the whole (Etzioni, 1996, 1997). Principled decentralization, when accompanied by layered loyalties, embodies the metaphor mosaic in practice.

To these metaphors I would add the metaphor of neighborhoods within a city to help us think about how nesting of communities within a broader community would work in schools. Imagine, for example, a 750-student elementary school in Toronto for grades 1–6. There are five sections of each grade in this school. The school is organized into five "families," each consisting of one set of grades located in its own area and designed to keep the same 150 youngsters and 6 teachers together as a "school within a school" through all six of their school years. The five families share the cafeteria, library, and other school facilities, abide by a few general schoolwide rules, and participate in some schoolwide traditions. At the same time, each of the families operates like an independent learning community or school within this larger school.

Though they share common elements, the families are unique in important ways. One of the families is a French-immersion school. The second has adopted the Basic School Principles as an organizing framework for planning and organizing the curriculum. A third family emphasizes Caribbean-Canadian themes in its humanities curriculum and uses the Constitution, the Charter of Rights and Freedoms, and other documents as a framework for developing a constitutional society that guides how they will live their lives together. Still another family relies heavily on learning exhibitions, project learning, and other progressive ideas. In this family the same teachers stay with the same youngsters for the first three years of their schooling, a pattern repeated in grades 4–6 as well. A fifth family spends Tuesdays and Thursdays visiting museums, conducting surveys, studying neighborhoods, engaging in scientific investigations in local streams, and using the community as a classroom. This family believes that schooling without walls is both motivating to students and pedagogically sound. The five families differ in how they handle the details of discipline, what subjects get emphasized, how the work of students is assessed, and other important matters. While some learning outcomes are the same across all five families, other learning outcomes differ family by family.

Each of the five families functions, much as does a neighborhood in a city, by celebrating its unique purposes, habits, traditions, work patterns, and culture. As parts of a mosaic they bring different colors and hues to the school. But they are also integral and interdependent parts of a whole that shares values and commitments. All of the "neighborhoods" in this school are bound by certain beliefs: all students can learn if they try and if teachers work hard, virtues must be institutionalized into the school culture, teachers are members of communities of practice, parents should accept their responsibility for helping the school work, students are entitled to unconditional acceptance and have important contributions to make, respect is a standard that applies equally to everyone, form should follow function when making decisions, character education is important, and so on. Though each of the families adopts a different curriculum and a different pedagogy, all five families are expected to engage students in authentic learning. The curriculum itself must be constructivist without compromising attention to basic skills of literacy and numeracy.

This list of common standards might be prefaced by two or three schoolwide rules such as no fighting, no drugs, and no weapons. These commonalities seem sufficient to ensure that, despite similarities that might exist within school families (communities) and differences that might exist between them, ample guarantees are provided that ensure levels of civility, decency, and respect for everyone. Though layered, shared ideas and moral authority remain the reason for what goes on within the larger school. At the center of this moral authority are shared conceptions about individual rights of community members and their responsibilities to the larger good.

Eight conditions seem necessary for community theory to evolve in this direction:

1. Schools need to be redefined as collections of people and ideas rather than as structures of brick and mortar. Thus within any school building many independent and semi-independent schools might exist side by side.

2. Shared values that lead to the development of tightly knit communities of mind and heart need to be encouraged within schools, while at the same time respect for the defining differences that make a school unique need to be encouraged between schools. The goal should be to create communities nested within communities, neighborhoods within cities, and schools within schools across the educational landscape.

3. Though some schools might function as schools within schools and others as free-standing schools connected to a larger complex of schools, all schools need to be tied together by common foundational values.

4. Layered loyalties to one's own school community and to the larger community of schools needs to be cultivated.

5. Nothing in the concepts of nested communities, neighborhoods within a city, or schools within a school should compromise the individual rights of students, parents, teachers, and other community members.

6. This emphasis on individual rights needs to be tempered by deliberately linking rights to responsibilities within a framework of commitment to civic virtue, defined as the willingness of each member of the community, individually and collectively, to sacrifice their self-interest on behalf of the common good.

7. Within practical limits, students and their families, as well as teachers, should be able to choose the particular school, school family, or school within a school they wish to join. This "school" of choice should be part of a larger legal framework of school or schools and resourced at an equitable level.

8. Commitment to both individual rights and shared responsibilities that are connected to the common good should provide the basis for moral leadership.

5

Layered Standards and Shared Accountability

B uilding diverse and effective school communities that focus on both caring and competence is a good idea. But we have a problem. We can't have this kind of community and a standards movement that imposes on all schools the same expectations and the same outcomes for learning. The present standards movement needs to be realigned. If we continue with standardized standards and assessment then we place community building at risk and compromise the lifeworlds of parents, teachers, students, and local communities. We can avoid this problem by switching to layered standards and shared accountability. Both can accelerate the building of effective school communities. By switching we can have our cake and eat it, too.

Changing Our Course

Switching our approach to standards is not the same as doing away with standards. Setting standards for what students need to know, for what levels of civility should characterize student behavior, for what schools need to do, and for how parents, teachers, and even governors and legislators define their roles with respect to educational issues is good for students, schools, and the country. Standards are most useful when they are accompanied by assessments that can be used to determine where we are with respect to our goals and to help us get better. Personally, I like standards and assessments, if we have the right kind. Both can help us to define the common good and to come together in a quest to pursue that good. Standards and assessments can play an important role in building the kinds of focused and caring school communities most Americans want.

As now construed, however, standards colonize rather than enhance the lifeworld of schools, place schools' organizational character at risk, compromise their responsiveness to local needs and aspirations, hamper effective teaching and learning, and frustrate attempts to instill learning and caring virtues in students. Changing our present approach, however, will not be easy. We seem to be in the middle of another fad stampede, and stampedes have a way of spoiling good ideas.

When a stampede hits our classrooms, directions change with such force that we get herd-like swings in educational policy and practice from the statehouse to the schoolhouse. This is what is happening with the standards movement. Unlike normal, thoughtful changes that incrementally alter existing practices over time, stampedes are accompanied by rapid commitment to a new course of action that has a habit of compromising rationality (Staw, 1984). Continuing to raise the bar by tightening standards and assessments as student failure rates increase is one example. Another is assuming that centralizing standards and assessments at the state level in large states such as Texas, California, or New York is local control. Still another is raising standards without providing the resources and training needed for teachers to teach at higher academic levels.

The standards stampede, for example, is rapidly becoming a "one best way" prescription for school improvement that seeks to determine what must be learned and at what minimal level this learning should take place, regardless of local traditions, values, needs, and interests. It is almost as if what students, parents, teachers, and communities are interested in and think important does not count.

Standards advocates are quick to point out that parents, teachers, testing experts, politicians, and corporate leaders are typically represented on state-appointed committees charged with writing or jurying standards. But the vast majority of ordinary people do not have a direct role or say in this process. In my view it may be okay to decide whether a new highway should run from east to west rather than west to east by representative government, but when the issues have to do with our children—their social and mental health, their civic and intellectual development, and their spiritual and moral growth—then we need democratic government in the form of direct participation of those affected by the issues. Unquestionably the state has an important role in this process. And unquestionably so do parents, teachers, students, and other citizens in local school communities. Granted there are some things that everyone should learn, but there are also some things that might be learned by some people but not by others.

Ends Determine the Means

Because ends, in the form of standardized standards and assessments, ultimately determine means, the further we move in the direction of specifying standards across the curriculum and then testing to see if these standards have been met, the more likely we will be to determine the details of the curriculum to be taught and the kinds of teaching needed for it to be learned. This, then, provides a central agency with virtually complete control of the educational process. Who controls what and how has direct consequences for the kind of profession teaching will become and for the lifeworlds of individual teachers. If a vital lifeworld is needed in every individual school to provide the character, discretion, sense of community, motivation, and commitment that teachers and students need to be responsive and effective, then we have to worry about across-the-board standards and assessments.

High Stakes or Wrong Stakes?

Of further concern is that a standardized system is by its nature high stakes. This system determines which students will be winners and which students will be losers and what the consequences of winning and losing will be, not just for a day, semester, or year but in some cases for a lifetime. In some states if students can't demonstrate that they have mastered the official standards, a diploma will not be granted and post-high-school options are dramatically reduced.

Why is this situation worrisome? Because our standards and assessments are not infallible. I am thinking of two successful persons I know who are "self-made." One is a professor at a respected university and the other is a multimillionaire philanthropist with an interest in education. Each has a modest school record. One could be considered a late bloomer and the other could be considered as having "street smarts." I wonder what would have happened to them if they had had to successfully pass a standards-based exam to graduate from high school. Robert Sternberg tells the story about Jack, the "smartest" student in the class, and Irvin, who was often the butt of Jack's jokes. Jack routinely gave Irvin the choice of two coins, a nickel and a dime. To Jack's delight, Irvin always selected the nickel. When asked why, Irvin pointed out that if he chose the dime, Jack would not keep asking him to choose. "I've collected over a dollar so far[;] all I have to do is keep choosing the nickel" (Sternberg, 1996). Jack may well be meeting the school's standards, but Irvin, like my millionaire acquaintance, is meeting life's standards.

Standards or Judgments

The word *standard* can be intimidating and that causes problems as we try to redirect the standards movement. The dictionary defines a standard as a rule to measure the quality and quantity of something. A learning standard or school standard, to most ordinary citizens, is something similar to the gold standard—a scientific and objective measure of something valuable that ordinary people had better not mess with. Thus parents rarely ask what a standards-based, state-assigned school rating such as "exemplary" or "needs improvement" means. They just assume that whatever is being measured should be measured and whatever the ratings are, they must be scientific ones. If a standard is met, that is good. And if a standard is not met, then that is bad.

But standards are not scientific, fixed, or precise. They are subjective. Some standards are good and some are bad; some are measured properly and some are not. In some cases the rating scheme that evaluates the extent to which a standard is met is set too high. And in other cases it is set too low. Standards are not "scientifically analyzed" to determine if they have universal validity. Nor are they measured by something as precise and uncontroversial as a thermometer, vacuum pump, or pressure gauge. There is no *Le Grande K* that provides a universally fixed and sure metastandard against which other standards can be compared.

Instead, ordinary people, albeit with some knowledge of the field in question, make human decisions about these matters. When deciding on standards these people often differ. One group of people might prefer some standards, accept others, and reject still others. Another group may prefer, accept, and reject standards in the same field, but they may be different standards than those of individuals in the first group.

While conceding that there might be some controversy about standards in social studies and other "soft" areas, many readers assume that standard setting should be relatively noncontroversial and easy in areas such as math and science, or in basic skill areas. Diane Ravitch, arguing for a single set of national standards that would apply to all students, points out, for example, that "mathematics and science work according to the same principles regardless of the city, state, or nation. The airplane that just flew over my home doesn't care what country it is in; it works the same in Austria, Nigeria, and Japan as it does in the United States" (quoted in Olson, 1998, p. 25).

But, for example, in California the crafting of science standards by a state-appointed commission turned out to be a daunting task. The commission splintered into two major groups. One group, the Science Coalition, favored an inquiry approach that would help students think like scientists, experience science, learn general scientific principles, and be able to solve scientific problems. The other group, the Associated Scientists, favored a content acquisition approach and pushed for standards that were more graded, content-oriented, and amenable to direct instruction. One of the Associated Scientists commissioners stated that "the commissioners had profound differences in issues that go to the heart of education—instructional style, the appropriate age at which to introduce material, the best way to assess student learning, and the interpretation of research. Their frequent clashes were rooted in fundamental disagreements over what and how children should learn" (Olson, 1998, p. 28).

In the end the commissioners struck a compromise that neither side celebrated but both sides could live with. Once the commission's work was done, it was up to the California State Board of Education to decide whether to accept the compromise package or some other combination of standards. The board approved standards that reflected the views of the more traditional commissioners. The new standards specify what students should learn at every grade, with scientific inquiry and problem solving taking a clear back seat to content per se (Hoff, 1998b). So much for viewing educational standards as akin to the gold standard!

What about a skill area such as reading? Wouldn't that area be safe from controversy? In 1993 the U.S. Department of Education commissioned the National Council of Teachers of English, the International Reading Association, and the Center for the Study of Reading at the University of Illinois at Urbana-Champaign to develop and recommend national standards. When the draft standards were proposed, the Department of Education rejected the work and subsequently terminated funding. One of the drafters of the standards explained the rejection as follows: "the standards were excessively concerned with 'process' and insufficiently concerned with 'products' or 'outcomes'" (Clinchy, 1995, p. 11). It seems clear that where reading is concerned different ideologies lead to different conclusions. Setting standards, under these circumstances, can resemble a game of winning and losing rather than scientific inquiry into a discipline or a skill field to determine some sort of truth. Standards are subjective reflections of the preferences of those who set them. Different people set different standards. The process is as much political as it is anything else. If you want standards that you will like, assign the task of setting standards to people you agree with.

Assessing standards is equally subjective. For assessment purposes standards have to be converted into performance indicators. Sometimes formal tests are used that yield right and wrong answers that can be scored by numerically weighted responses. Other times rubrics are used to sort responses into performance levels such as basic, proficient, or advanced. Experts examine the work students do using the rubrics and provide a rating—a process that makes a lot of sense but still has a lot of problems.

The 1994 National Assessment of Educational Progress (NAEP), for example, applies "basic," "proficient," and "advanced" ratings to student achievement. Many advocates and critics of American schools use these test scores as evidence that schools are either doing okay or are not doing very well and need to be overhauled. A lot depends on the particular scores that the critics pay attention to and how they interpret these scores. In 1994, for example, NAEP found that about 40 percent of fourth graders tested could not read at the "basic" level, as defined by certain score ranges. To the average citizen that means that 40 percent of our fourth graders cannot read! But what NAEP intended to communicate was that students could read all right, but just not up to the level that was required to earn the "basic" designation. The basic designation was determined by a group of teachers who were assembled by NAEP to rate the difficulty of the exam questions and the caliber of student responses. Had it been a different group, a different level would likely have been set.

James Pellegrin, who chairs the National Assessment Governing Board, points out that "the standards are based on judgments by experts and don't reflect some deep truths" (Hoff, 1998a, p. 23). Many informed groups, including testing experts at the General Accounting Office, which is the research arm of Congress, believe that the NAEP scoring ranges were pegged too high, thus yielding lower scores than students might have gotten from taking the Advanced Placement Exam or some similar exam for the same subject matter. The point is that educational standards are well short of being gold standards and so are our scoring rubrics and our rating levels. Should we still use them? Of course, but we should view the information as information that can help us understand and plan and not as objective statements of summary judgments.

I believe our present system of standards and assessments is salvageable. We have the ingredients we need to develop an approach that will work for both the state's legitimate interests and the local schools' need to protect and grow its own unique lifeworld. All we need to do is put the parts together differently. But before we continue, let's take a close look at standards and testing in one state, Texas, and see what we can learn.

Despite Good Intentions

The testing situation in Texas provides an example of how systemsworld applications designed to serve one set of purposes and ideals may wind up serving another. A good accountability system, for example, should be designed to help us find out the extent to which students are learning what they, their parents, and teachers think should be learned. Further, test data and other information can help parents, teachers, and students plan better and be more effective in achieving goals, hopes, and dreams. These are great intentions. But, unfortunately, the accountability system falls short.

Though Texas' policymakers may intend differently, the state's accountability system determines which goals are important for each

school in the state and which goals are not important. The accountability system also regulates how teachers and principals behave and
many aspects of the individual lifeworlds of students. The Texas
example is by no means unusual. Many other states and some countries function similarly.

Texas is often cited as a state with a model accountability system. Students are tested by the state regularly in reading, writing,
and math to assess their mastery of the essential elements and skills
for these areas as embodied in the state curriculum. Each school in
the state is sorted into one of four categories (exemplary, recognized,
acceptable, or low performing) based on the scores of its students.
There is enormous pressure to receive at least an acceptable rating.
Low-performing schools are not only named in the press but also
subject to formal sanctions.

Some educators report being under pressure to maintain high
ratings once they are achieved. An exemplary rating, for example,
may be a mixed blessing. This rating raises expectations to the point
that superintendents and parents often consider it the minimum.
Anything lower than exemplary is, thus, considered low performing. Principals are typically evaluated by their superintendents in
terms of how well their schools do on the tests, and they feel personally responsible to avoid ratings that will displease their superintendents. The Texas principal evaluation system recommended
for use in local school districts by the Texas Commissioner of Education, for example, places primary emphasis on how well students
have done on required state tests. This test score emphasis puts
enormous pressure on principals that becomes pressure on teachers
that becomes pressure on students.

Tests are given in grades 3, 4, 5, 8, 9, and 10. All sections of the
10th-grade test (the exit test) must be passed before a student can
graduate, regardless of how well she or he might do on other performance indicators. A student, for example, might successfully
complete a challenging service requirement, pull an A in several
courses, be student president, win an essay contest, be a debate team

leader, save a life by applying first aid techniques learned in health class, and play in the school orchestra, but if she or he can't manage a 70 on the math portion of the exit exam, graduation with a traditional diploma is denied.

A school's rating is based on the percentage of its students who pass the required tests, not on absolute scores. Thus a school that manages to get 90 percent of its students barely passing with a grade of 70 can be rated higher than another school with fewer students passing but with much higher scores—let's say scores in the high 80s and 90s. Some exemplary schools, as a result, could be fairly mediocre given the state's criteria, while some mediocre schools could have large numbers of exemplary students. Many schools, as a result, are more concerned with the number of students they can get above the minimum than they are with getting exceptional student work. Only 45 percent of the tested students must pass for the school to receive at least an acceptable rating. To the state's credit, emphasis is given to attendance and dropout rates and to how well students in all racial and ethnic categories do. Further, the 45 percent passing figure will likely be increased progressively. The commissioner of education mentions 70 percent as the passing rate by the year 2004.

The tests are high stakes not only because low-performing schools are subject to sanctions but because of the state's policy to encourage local employers not to hire students whose grades and test scores are poor. The state commissioner of education, for example, makes it a point to regularly admonish employers who fail to consider test scores and grades as part of the employment decisions they make. Further, since all three sections of the 10th-grade exit test must be passed before a student can graduate with a traditional diploma, students fear being denied access to college or to employment opportunities. A student who gets a high of 69 on the math portion of the exit test after several attempts might have the grades, the physical ability, the interest, and a passing score on all application exams for the Marine Corps or the local college, but he or she cannot get into either without that diploma.

Colonization of the lifeworld by the systemsworld not only erodes school character, but individual character as well. It is common, for example, for administrators and teachers to group their students into three categories, depending on how well they have performed on past tests. One category is composed of students who are likely to pass the test (at least get a score of 70) without additional help. A second category includes students who are perceived as not likely to pass the test without unusual amounts of help or regardless of the help they receive. The third category is composed of "bubble students." These are the students whose previous test scores ranged from 60–69 and who, with intensive tutoring, are thought likely to get at least a 70 during the next testing period. In many schools, students in the first two groups receive far less attention and are allocated fewer resources than are provided to the bubble students. As part of this intensification, particularly for the bubble students, the curriculum is skewed in the direction of those skill areas that are most likely to be tested.

Many Texas schools have adopted various approaches to teaching and learning and various models of schooling that provide a sense of purpose and coherence to their work. Expeditionary Learning, Core Knowledge, Success for All, Accelerated Learning, and the Basic School are but a few examples of some well-known models that are used by these schools. Other schools invent models of their own. By adopting or inventing a model, schools hope to bring about a vision and purpose that unites parents, teachers, and students—a development that can grow character, build community, and make the school more effective in the long run. The Basic School, for example, believes in a coherent curriculum that includes study in such fields as language, history, science, literature, civics, and health. Fields are organized thematically and are integrated in the way in which they are studied. Since most of the models are frameworks and not scripts, teachers are drawn together into high levels of collegiality as they work to turn the frameworks into operational curriculum and pedagogy. Instead of enhancing this lifeworld view of schooling, the state's systemsworld accountability requirements wind up determining the vision.

Texas' testing has brought to many schools a seasonal cycle that goes something like this. Begin the school year being faithful to what you believe about schooling, your purposes, your shared vision, and other commitments that you make to students. This is a relatively long season that begins in September and normally runs through the remainder of that calendar year. Beginning in the second semester there is a gradual movement away from one's school vision and other lifeworld concerns toward addressing the demands of the tests. Tests are given in April. By late February or early March the focus on tests reaches a frenzy in some schools. Many of the things that schools wind up doing as they prepare their students for the tests contradict the values and beliefs that are defined in their missions. Basic schools, for example, simply cannot afford to spend very much time on integrating their curriculum thematically when what counts is the percentage of their students who will score a 70 or higher on the reading, math, and writing tests. Further, narrowing the focus of the curriculum to what will be tested risks neglecting the substance of history, social studies, art, and other disciplines.

May begins still another season. With the testing over in April, one notices a discernible slip as neither teachers nor students seem tuned in to the defining conceptions of schooling that dominated the first semester (the basic school model, for example) or the intensification of focus and drill that dominates the second semester. As one principal put it recently, "Once the tests are over the teachers and kids just coast to the finish line no matter what I say or do. We essentially waste the last four or five weeks of schooling."

The standards and assessment stampede in America should not surprise us. Ours is, after all, a technical-rational society that honors the maxim "If you can't measure it, it doesn't have value." As educators we have a special responsibility to point out the difficulties of this position and to re-evaluate our present rush to standardization and assessment. As William Spady (1998) points out:

In America, test scores are us. And they'd better be "good," even if no one can explain what an individual score "means" in terms of precisely defined student capabilities, or which score clearly differentiates competence from incompetence.

Consequently, America's teachers are doing exactly what is "rational" if they want to keep their jobs: focusing exclusively and obsessively on the things that will probably be on the test, and drilling students over and over on that narrow range of things until they memorize it [p. 38].

Spady proposes twelve questions that teachers and principals can use to quiz policymakers, corporate executives, fellow educators, and others who are caught up in the stampede (see Spady, 1998, p. 38). Among them are

- What does this test actually measure?

- What does this test not measure?

- What does this test not measure that is important to students' success in the information age?

- Why don't we measure and report that instead?

- What does a particular student test score mean?

- Does this one test score represent the student's total learning and achievement?

- Which score on this test indicates a student is competent?

- Does one point less indicate that the student is incompetent?

Standards have the potential to provide needed focus and to rally our resources in a common direction. Testing is a powerful tool that can help us assess how well standards are being achieved. Both can provide clues as to how we can get better. If standards and testing per se are not the issue, what is? The issue is colonization of the lifeworld by the systemsworld. *Instead of standards and accountability being derived from the needs, purposes, and interests of parents, teachers, and students in each school, the standards and accountability systems determine what the needs, purposes, and interests are and scripts the behavior of teachers and students accordingly.* When the lifeworld dominates, testing reflects local passions, needs, values, and beliefs. Standards remain rigorous and true but are not standardized. While tests possess the proper psychometric properties and the integrity of their substance is maintained, the test specifics reflect local values and preferences. Further, the worth of individuals in schools is not determined by some narrow definition of effectiveness and achievement, but by a range of assessments that responds to both local and state visions and needs.

Layered Standards as an Alternative

Colonization of the lifeworld by the systemsworld in the area of standards and accountability has serious negative long-term effects on a school's culture, character, and performance. Both uniqueness and discretion at the school site are needed for a school's culture and character to flourish. Both are compromised by the present "one best way" system of accountability that Texas and many other states now share. Is the answer to do away with standards, accountability, and other systemsworld applications? No, I don't think so. Schools work well when both the systemsworld and the lifeworld are expressed together. With the lifeworld being at the center, this means crafting systems of standards and accountability that serve the lifeworld rather than dominate it.

Can such a system be created? Yes, if we are willing to adopt a layered approach to establishing standards and a shared approach to accountability that includes a strong local component. Yes, if we are willing to abandon thinking in terms of a one best way to do things. Yes, if we are able to commit ourselves to the value of *mutuality* in an effort to bring together the state, the local school district, and individual schools as partners in search of a common good.

Mutuality is an important concept in a democratic society. (See the discussion of mutuality in Chapter One.) It implies the authentic "sharing of power-with, by, and among members in a society in a way that recognizes the fundamental dignity of each and the obligation to attain and maintain for each what is necessary to sustain that dignity" (Nothwehr, 1998b, p. 233). In educational societies, for example, states count but not more than students, parents, teachers, and other local members. Indeed the state's primary role in mutuality is to accept the obligation for ensuring the dignity of all participants. In high-stakes decision making, maintaining the dignity of all invested parties requires the adoption of a "power-with" standard. Nothwehr (1998a) cites Heyward (1989) as follows: "Power is the ability to move, effect, make a difference; the energy to create or destroy; put for or put down. . . . Power can be used for good or for ill. Using power-with others is good. Using power-over others is evil" (p. 191). A layered system of standards and shared accountability is an example of power-with.

Let's summarize with some assumptions:

- It is perfectly reasonable for the state to participate in setting standards for the schools. It is equally reasonable for school boards, parents, and teachers at the local school, and even students, to participate in setting standards, too. We just have to figure out who has responsibility for what.
- When standards and assessments are set by the state alone, standardization is likely to emerge, with schools becoming more and

more similar as a result. When school boards, parents, teachers, and students at the local school level participate in setting standards and determining assessments, schools become standardized in some few areas but diverse in most other areas.

• The advantage of a standards setting and assessment system that combines some common understandings with many diverse understandings is that it is consistent with the American democratic ideal, honors diversity, and provides the basis for real choice.

• Choice in itself is an empty idea. It only has meaning when students and parents are provided with different options to choose from. Providing real choices requires creating new programs and new images of schools. This is hard to do unless schools have responsibility for setting most of the standards they will pursue, for participating in the assessment of those standards, and for making this information public.

• The state should assume major responsibility for developing standards and assessments for all schools in the skill areas of reading, math, and writing.

• The school board, parents, teachers, and students at the local school level should share responsibility for developing standards and assessments in advanced math, science, literature, history, social science, art, music, English, and other areas. Since school districts and schools within them differ, it should be expected that many of these standards will differ as one moves from district to district and from school to school.

• Since the abilities and dispositions of parents, teachers, and students at the local school level vary with respect to how to write standards and how to craft assessments, the state has a responsibility to provide both technical assistance and financial resources for professional development.

• The state has a responsibility to provide a centralized standards bank from which local authorities might draw as needed. Some local authorities may choose to use standards from this bank "as is," and others might choose to use standards from this bank as frameworks for creating their own standards. It should be expected that different standards reflecting unique local values, needs, and purposes will be developed.

• Students should participate by setting standards for themselves and by assessing their own performance. Student assessments should count, along with state, school district, and local school assessments, in evaluating a school.

• No single set of standards and no single assessment system should dominate the other. If it is decided that schools must be rated and compared with each other (an idea I personally do not support), then no single rating source should determine a school's score or a school's category designation (that is, exemplary, recognized, acceptable, needs improvement).

In the next chapter I propose that, in addition to layered standards and shared accountability, the scope of evaluating schools needs to be expanded to include an array of quality indicators that go beyond specifying outcomes and measuring results. I explore, also, the possibility of introducing a version of "whole school inspection" as a way to operationalize layered standards and expand the scope of school evaluation. Whatever direction we take, it must be guided by the following principle: "The child is not the mere creature of the state; those who nurture him and direct his destiny [parents and teachers, for example] have the right, coupled with the high duty, to recognize and prepare him for additional obligation" (*Pierce v. Society of Sisters*, 1925, p. 268).

6

Whole Child, Whole School, Holistic Assessment

W hat we want are good schools. We want to be able to identify the ones we have, learn from them, and increase their
number. We want good schools and all other schools to get even
better. We want to provide schools and their publics with information as to where they are now, given their own goals and aspirations,
those of the state, and those of other legitimate interests. We want
them to use this information to plan next steps, new directions, and
other events on the road to improvement. But we can't do any of
these things well unless we get involved in assessment. And getting
involved in assessment means having a good, practical, broad, realistic, and lifeworld-serving definition of what a good school is in the
first place.

More Than Effective

It is much easier to nail down what an effective school is than to
struggle with a broader definition of *good school*. Sara Lawrence
Lightfoot's research, reported in her book *The Good High School*
(1983), is a good example of searching for a meaningful and expansive definition of effectiveness. She provides portraits of six very different but good high schools. What emerges from this seminal study
is that a single list or a single set of indicators for a good school is not
so easily achieved. Good schools are rich and diverse. Her portraits

reveal images of schools that uniquely serve different neighborhoods, contain a unique mix of goals and purposes, use unique ways to achieve these goals and purposes, and have principals who provide a unique blend of leadership strategies and styles. Goodness is about the kind of wholeness in purpose and responsiveness to unique characteristics and needs that builds school character. Goodness builds from and grows a school's lifeworld.

In Texas, by contrast, a de facto definition of an effective school is a school that gets the right rating based on the state's accountability tests. Paradoxically, Texas has a broad commitment to "learner-centered" schools and even has developed learner-centered proficiencies for preparing teachers and administrators to practice in learner-centered schools, the characteristics of which resemble many of those found by Lightfoot in her search for good schools. But when push comes to shove, everyone knows that it is not the learner-centered proficiencies but having the right rating and the right scores that counts—a development too common among other states and in the United Kingdom, and in other countries as well.

Defining a good school isn't easy, and maybe that's why policymakers avoid trying. Yet intuitively "goodness" is a known quality no matter how difficult it is to define precisely and to measure adequately. Joan Lipsitz (1984), for example, found that the principals of the good schools she studied had difficulty articulating what it was that made their schools special or what the dimensions of goodness were. "You will have to come and see my school" was the typical and predictable response of these principals to questions about goodness.

We know good schools when we experience them, although we cannot always specify with precision their components. We know that in good schools things "hang together," a sense of purpose rallies people to a common cause, work has meaning and life is significant, teachers and students work together with spirit, and accomplishments are readily recognized. To say that good schools have high morale or achieve higher test scores or send more students to college, and leave it at that, is to miss the point. Goodness is all of this and even more (see Sergiovanni, 1995).

Parents, too, have broad conceptions of what a good school is. True, most surveys indicate that basic skill learning and developing fundamental academic competence are paramount goals in their minds. But when parents are pushed a bit further, most provide a more expansive view of school success. The goals they talk about include developing a love of learning, critical-thinking and problem-solving skills, aesthetic appreciation, curiosity and creativity, and interpersonal competence. Though they are likely to be very unhappy if their children have not mastered "the basics," parents want a complete education for their children (see Goodlad, 1983).

Some Characteristics of Good Schools

In reviewing the literature on effectiveness and goodness, Duttweiler (1990) concludes that good schools can be generally described as being student-centered. They make an effort to serve all students, create support networks to assist students, involve students in school affairs, respect and celebrate the ethnic and linguistic differences among students, and place student welfare first. Good schools also offer academically rich programs that emphasize higher-order as well as lower-order cognitive objectives, provide an enriched environment, have an active cocurricular program, provide in-depth coverage of content, and appropriately monitor student progress by providing necessary feedback.

Duttweiler also notes that good schools provide a distinctive normative structure that supports teaching and learning. They believe all students can learn and feel responsible for seeing that they do, believe in their ability to influence student learning, design programs to ensure academic success, communicate expectations to students, provide focused and organized teaching, adapt teaching to student needs, head off academic problems, anticipate and correct student misconceptions, and use a variety of teaching strategies. Further, teaching takes place within a positive school climate characterized by a sense of order, purpose, and direction fostered by consistency among teachers, an atmosphere of encouragement, and a work-centered, open, friendly, and culturally inviting environment.

Good schools also foster collegial interaction by creating professional environments that facilitate the work of teachers. Teachers participate in making decisions affecting their work, share a sense of purpose and community, receive recognition, and are treated with respect and dignity by others in the workplace. Good schools have extensive staff development that emphasizes the exchange of practical teaching techniques and that makes learning an integral part of a collaborative educational environment. They practice a shared leadership by respecting teachers as professionals, emphasizing solving problems through collaboration, and involving staff in critical aspects of the school, including developing goals, values, and a mission. Good schools foster creative problem solving and make a habit of turning the problems they face into challenges. They engage in solving problems with commitment, creativity, persistence, and professionalism. Finally, Duttweiler found that good schools involve parents in the life of the school.

In seeking to identify indicators of school goodness, MacBeath, Boyd, Rand, and Bell (1995) asked 638 respondents affiliated with ten schools in England and Wales to provide their own indicators of a good school. Six primary schools, three secondary schools, and one special school were involved in the survey. Respondents included pupils, teachers, parents, members of the school management team, support staff, and governors or school board members. The respondents generated 1,743 different criteria and more than three hundred individual lists. Each of the lists was unique in that no two people had the same five items worded in exactly the same way.

Though each list had its own internal logic and expressed its own value system, common themes and issues specific to a particular role could be identified. As MacBeath and his associates (1995) explain, "This can be illustrated by the following six examples from a teacher, a pupil, a parent, a member of support staff, a governor [school board member], and a member of the senior management team. It shows issues held in common and issues specific to a particular standpoint. These are chosen as *fairly typical examples* of what people wrote when asked to give their own five indicators of a good school" (p. 21). The responses are summarized in Exhibit 6.1.

What is fascinating about the responses is that there are many definitions of a good school. Certainly there are overlaps among the six perspectives, but still people in different roles have different views about what is important—all views that count in a good school evaluation.

Academic results are important, but each of the six groups of stakeholders believes that a good school is something larger and more significant than a school that gets "good results." Process counts, so does climate, and so do other, related concerns. The responses of parents in particular are interesting. For them a good school is a good place for their children to be. It is a welcome, caring, well-disciplined place where people invest time in children and where relationships between teachers and parents are good.

Other descriptions of good schools are as follows:

• MacBeath and his colleagues (1995) point out that "If we could talk of a 'parent perspective' it is one which puts personal development and growth at the centre" (p. 26).

• Barry McGaw and his colleagues in Australia report: "Above all, they (parents) want schools in which students learn to think well of themselves, to develop a sense of personal value and a confidence in themselves to take them into adult life. They want competition but they want it to be with a student's past performance not with the performance of other students" (cited in MacBeath and others, 1995, p. 26).

• A 1989 study of parents' views in Scotland (MacBeath) echoes these sentiments with the words of one parent: "What I want for my children is to be what they can be, to feel at the end

**Exhibit 6.1. Indicators of a Good School:
Six Composite Perspectives.**

Pupil

- Pupils are nice to each other.
- Everyone is treated fairly.
- There is a friendly atmosphere.
- Teachers control the classes but are not too strict.
- Teachers help you with things you are not good at.

Teacher

- Communication is good among all members.
- Staff development is good.
- The environment is good to work in (buildings, repairs, presentation).
- Pupils are happy and well motivated.
- All pupils are helped to achieve what they're capable of.

Parent

- There is a welcoming friendly atmosphere.
- Staff are caring and communicate well with pupils.
- Discipline is good.
- Extra time is spent with children who learn less quickly.
- Relationships are good between teachers and parents.

Management

- Pupils feel safe.
- All members of the school community work toward clear objectives.
- A high quality of information is given to parents and visitors.
- Rules are applied evenly and fairly.
- All pupils are helped to achieve what they're capable of.

Support Staff

- Resources are good and up to date.
- Classrooms are clean, warm, and comfortable.
- Support staff are given credit for their competence and contribution.
- The environment is friendly and welcoming.
- Staff development involves all staff.

Exhibit 6.1. Indicators of a Good School:
Six Composite Perspectives, cont'd.

Governor (Board Member, Trustee)

- Excellent reputation with the local community.
- Strong leadership from senior management.
- A happy and welcoming environment.
- Pupils being helped to reach their individual potential.
- A safe place for pupils and teachers.

The respondents were given an open-ended question, "What, in your view, are the key characteristics of a 'good' school?" Adults and secondary school students were given a five-blank form on which to respond. Older primary students were simply asked to provide their own lists. Younger primary students were asked to draw or paint good or bad things about the school. There were 181 secondary school student respondents and 201 primary school student respondents.

Source: MacBeath, J., Boyd, B., Rand, J., and Bell, S. (1995). *Schools Speak for Themselves: Toward a Framework for Self-evaluation.* London: The National Union of Teachers, p. 21.

of their schooling, 'Well, I've got all I can out of school and now I can choose where I can go from here.' I want them to feel confident enough to be able to choose because they have to make the decisions, and the decisions they make on leaving school will have ripples throughout the rest of their life" (cited in MacBeath and others, 1995, p. 26).

MacBeath and his colleagues were able to synthesize the 1,743 different criteria that they received from their 638 respondents into ten general indicators or characteristics of a good school. These are summarized in Exhibit 6.2.

MacBeath and his colleagues (1995) point out that when schools develop their own criteria for self-evaluation they are engaged in an exercise that is quite different from when criteria are provided by researchers or policymakers. Self-evaluation is concerned with not just student needs but the needs of teachers, parents, and others as

Exhibit 6.2. Ten General Indicators: What Key Stakeholders Consider to Be the Characteristics of a Good School.

1. *School Climate*

   At the center lies school climate because that was mentioned most often by all groups. The words *atmosphere*, *climate*, or *ethos* were often used specifically, more so by teachers and parents and less so by secondary students and hardly at all by primary pupils. They did refer, however, to the school as a friendly place and made allusions to how a school "is" or "feels." We have included all of these within the category of "school climate."

2. *Relationships*

   We have put "relationships" into a separate category because they were mentioned frequently and specifically as determining characteristics of a good school. The most common form of relationship mentioned was student-teacher relationships, but staff were just as likely to mention collegial relationships, and relationships between teaching and support staff or between teaching staff and senior management.

3. *Classroom Climate*

   There were few direct references to "classroom climate" as such, but students in particular described ways in which classrooms were stimulating or interesting places. This category includes ways in which teachers set the conditions for "making lessons fun" or varied.

4. *Support for Learning*

   Ultimately everyone and everything in the school should focus on supporting young people in their learning. We have "support for learning" as a category on its own because, much more than any other group, pupils made specific reference to factors that helped them learn—and factors that hindered learning.

5. *Support for Teaching*

   For teachers, home-school links were important for supporting teaching, but reference was also made to a much wider set of conditions that supported the teacher. Some had to do with time and resources, some with relationships, and some referred to staff development time. Items in this category referred to helping the teacher function more effectively in the classroom. We have included class size, working conditions, and school infrastructure in this category.

6. *Time and Resources*

   The efficiency of organization and communication in the school bear some relationship to resources. Time is a critical resource that is deployed well or badly. Mention was made (more often by students than other groups) of "materials," "equipment," and opportunities and time to use them.

Exhibit 6.2. Ten General Indicators: What Key Stakeholders Consider to Be the Characteristics of a Good School, cont'd.

7. *Organization and Communication*

School climate and relationships are obviously affected by organization and communication in the school. We have made this a category on its own because of references made (more so by staff than any other group) to the efficiency of communication among staff and between staff and senior management.

8. *Equity*

We have used the term equity to cover a range of meanings. Equity referred to the school's openness to disabled people and the opportunity to succeed for those who had special needs. It referred to being treated equally, regardless of gender or race or academic ability. For pupils it very often meant being treated fairly and not being picked on by teachers.

9. *Recognition of Achievement*

Student achievement is, for most people, the chief purpose of the school, but it also meant recognizing and rewarding effort and excellence in a range of different ways. Criteria suggested by all groups emphasized the value of this as all-inclusive rather than for a select few. Under this heading we have included recognition of staff achievement, too, because it was mentioned a number of times in conjunction with student achievement as a hallmark of the genuinely positive and rewarding climate.

10. *Home-School Links*

Equity and achievement were issues that, perhaps more than any others, crossed the home-school divide, because schools have to be careful not to compound the failure of children already disadvantaged by home and community background. We have used this category to describe all references to parental involvement, to exchange of information between home and school, and to mentions of support and partnership.

Source: MacBeath, J., Boyd, B., Rand, J., and Bell, S. (1995). *Schools Speak for Themselves: Toward a Framework for Self-evaluation.* London: The National Union of Teachers, pp. 28–29.

well. It is about a range of things that affect pupil achievement, but it is more than pupil achievement. It is about numbers and scores, but it is also about people. "It is less concerned with norms and averages than with individuals and groups. What is important for an individual or small group may be seen as a priority for the school although that group or person is, in a statistical sense, insignificant. Keeping the needs of real young people, their families, and their teachers at the forefront was the message that came across to us in all the ten very different schools" (MacBeath and others, 1995, p. 28).

Taking Democracy Seriously

The situation in the United States and Canada is not very different from what we find in England and Wales. Schools here, too, have various publics who have important stakes in what goes on. Each of these groups has a legitimate interest in the schools—an interest that should not be easily washed away by majority rule and other procedural understandings of democracy. Democracy is first about substance—about values, principles, ideas, rights, responsibilities, and a sense of the common good. When the fate of one's own children is at stake, each individual should have a direct say. Naturally that say cannot ignore the larger public interest as the common good is defined and operationalized into school policies and practices. In some countries the rights of parents are so central to the educational process that they are even guaranteed constitutionally. Article 42.1 of the Irish Constitution, for example, acknowledges parents as the "primary and natural" educators of their children with a right to actively participate in their children's schooling and the right, as well, to be consulted and informed about all aspects of that schooling (Department of Education, Government of Ireland, 1996, p. 14).

Layered standards and shared accountability are ways to bring together individual and collective rights and responsibilities and local and state rights and responsibilities to benefit both individuals and society. This layered approach is a way to accommodate legitimate differences in a diverse society.

Are differences in what we want from schools real? Kernan-Schloss and Plattner (1998) point out that while today's parents and voters need to see signs of success if they are going to support schools, they do not agree on what the indicators of success are. Their polls and focus group discussions reveal that when citizens are asked, "What do you need to see that would indicate a school is getting better?" they get lots of different answers. Some citizens choose higher test scores, but others choose higher levels of parental engagement, improved safety and discipline, and smaller classes.

Kernan-Schloss and Plattner (1998), for example, recently asked a national sample of one thousand voters which of four indicators would tell them that schools were improving: parents personally involved in their children's education, increases in test scores and graduation rates, higher academic standards, and improved safety and discipline. Twenty-three percent of the respondents chose test scores, 19 percent higher standards, and 9 percent safety and discipline. At the same time, the authors point out, "When we asked which *major* changes they would implement, 25 percent chose teaching students values, such as tolerance, respect, and self-discipline; 23 percent chose raising academic requirements and standards so that students must prove themselves in order to graduate or advance a grade; 23 percent chose moving beyond the basics to problem solving and teamwork; and 22 percent chose requiring parents to take more active roles in the academic portion of their children's education" (p. 19).

All four of these changes were equally popular, but for different groups. College graduates, for example, favored raising standards while respondents with high school diplomas or less favored teaching values. Kernan-Schloss and Plattner (1998) conclude that the public is by no means monolithic. Nonetheless, policymakers and school officials who are advocates of across-the-board standards continue to think and act as if the public were monolithic. As a result, they continue to push for simplistic "one best way" solutions to the complex problem of improving schools through standards and other means. Appealing to the "democratic process" they often point out that a "one best way" is determined by having representatives from various groups of stakeholders vote on the various issues with the majority ruling. But democracy, particularly at the school level, is not the same as the National Football League, where winning and losing is routine. Many things, like school standards, should not be decided by voting. The majority should not always impose its will on others. Options and choices should be the democratic route to take. All schools should have high standards, but the standards need not all be the same.

Some Unanticipated Problems

When standards are applied across the board they wind up functioning as ends that drive the means. As a result, we run the risk of unduly narrowing the curriculum and of scripting teaching. Teachers focus almost exclusively on what will be tested, and their teaching is both direct and ritualistic. Many states note that they are respectful of local views by making their standards voluntary but, as is the case with California (Hoff, 1998b), they then announce that the state's accountability tests will be based on the content of these presumably voluntary standards.

These dysfunctions are symptoms of colonization of the lifeworlds of local schools, their parents, teachers, students, and other concerned local citizens. Systemsworld colonization of the lifeworld places the wrong people in the driver's seat. In an Education Commission of the States telephone survey, twenty-seven hundred parents were asked who has the most credibility about educational issues. Eighty-eight percent said teachers, 82 percent said the school children themselves, 82 percent said other parents, and 72 percent said local school officials (cited in Kernan-Schloss and Plattner, 1998, p. 20).

Here is the paradox. While parents value most the judgment of teachers, other parents, students, and local school officials, these groups have less and less to say about important matters of school-ing such as standards, outcomes, the curriculum, teaching, and as-sessment. Even the definition of what is a good school is provided by the state or, in some countries, the federal authorities. Localism counts, but then again it does not. It counts in rhetoric as politi-cians and policymakers talk about the sovereign rights of states but at the same time deny the rights of local communities within states.

Social and Emotional Learning

One of the limits to our present stampede in the direction of standards is that the goals and curriculum areas that will be emphasized are likely to be those most easily stated and measured as standards. This could result in the neglect of important learning and development areas that not only have intrinsic value but also have instrumental value. Such areas lead to more effective and efficient basic skills acquisition and to mastery of academic and related disciplines. The whole area of social and emotional learning (SEL) provides many examples (see Goleman, 1995; Sternberg and Wagner, 1995; Gardner, 1983, 1993).

> Social and emotional competence is the ability to under-stand, manage, and express the social and emotional aspects of one's life in ways that enable the successful management of life tasks such as learning, forming rela-tionships, solving everyday problems, and adapting to the complex demands of growth and development. It includes self-awareness, control of impulsivity, working cooperatively, and caring about oneself and others. Social and emotional learning is the process through which children and adults develop the skills, attitudes, and values necessary to acquire social and emotional competence [Elias and others, 1997, p. 2].

The full scope of what can be taught in an SEL-enriched cur-riculum (or left out in an SEL-deprived curriculum) is illustrated in Exhibit 6.3. This table depicts the Life Skills Curriculum Scope for

Exhibit 6.3. New Haven Social Development Curriculum Scope.

Life Skills Curriculum Scope
Preschool through 12th grade

Skills	Attitudes and Values
Self-Management	**About Self**
Self-monitoring	Self-respect
Self-control	Feeling capable
Stress management	Honesty
Persistence	Sense of responsibility
Emotion-focused coping	Willingness to grow
Self-reward	Self-acceptance
Problem Solving and Decision Making	**About Others**
Problem recognition	Awareness of social norms and values—peer,
Feelings awareness	family, community, and society
Perspective taking	Accepting individual differences
Realistic and adaptive goal setting	Respecting human dignity
Awareness of adaptive response strategies	Having concern or compassion for others
Alternative solution thinking	Valuing cooperation with others
Consequential thinking	Motivation to solve interpersonal problems
Decision making	Motivation to contribute
Planning	
Behavioral enactment	**About Tasks**
	Willingness to work hard
Communication	Motivation to solve practical problems
Understanding nonverbal communication	Motivation to solve academic problems
Sending messages	Recognition of the importance of education
Receiving messages	Respect for property
Matching communication to the situation	

Content

Self/Health	Relationships	School/Community
Alcohol and other drug use	Understanding relationships	Attendance education and truancy and dropout prevention
Education and prevention of AIDS and STDs	Multicultural awareness	Accepting and managing responsibility
Growth and development and teen pregnancy prevention	Making friends	Adaptive group participation
Nutrition	Developing positive relationships with peers of different genders, races, and ethnic groups	Realistic academic goal setting
Exercise	Bonding to prosocial peers	Developing effective work habits
Personal hygiene	Understanding family life	Making transitions
Personal safety and first aid	Relating to siblings	Environmental responsibility
Understanding personal loss	Relating to parents	Community involvement
Use of leisure time	Coping with loss	Career planning
Spiritual awareness	Preparation for marriage and parenting in later life	
	Conflict education and violence prevention	
	Finding a mentor	

Source: Elias, Zins, Weissberg, Frey, Greenberg, Haynes, Kessler, Schwab-Stone, and Shriver, 1997. Copyright © 1991 by Alice Stroop Jackson and Roger P. Weissberg.

preschool to 12th grade in the New Haven, Connecticut, schools (see Weissberg, Jackson, and Shriver, 1993). The goals of the curriculum are to help each student acquire knowledge, skills, work habits, and values for a lifetime of meaningful work; to motivate students to contribute responsively and effectively to their peer group, family, school, and community; to develop students' self-knowledge, self-worth, and ability to deal with daily responsibilities and challenges; to help students become socially skilled and have positive relationships with others; and to encourage students to engage in health protective behaviors. A short time ago these goals would have been considered frills, but in today's world they are essential not only to advancing school learning but also to succeeding in the work world and participating in the civic life of our society (see Elias and others, 1997, especially pp. 1–13).

An Assessment Approach

Howard Gardner (1993) believes that many of our problems with standards and accountability could be solved by taking an "assessment" rather than a "testing" approach. He defines assessment as obtaining information about the skills and potentials of students for the purposes of providing useful feedback to them and to the local community. Assessments obtain information naturally in a *situated context* and in the course of ordinary performances of teaching and learning. Tests, by contrast, are formal, artificial, and *decontextualized*.

To Gardner, assessments should be such a natural part of the educational process that they become indistinguishable from teaching and learning. Assessments have what Gardner calls "ecological validity" in the sense that they are validated by the content of learning itself. The process of teachers and students working closely and continuously together builds confidence in the teacher's ability to make sound assessment decisions. Further, "When individuals are assessed in situations which more closely resemble 'actual working conditions,' it is possible to make much better predictions about their ultimate performance. It is odd that most American school children spend hundreds of hours engaged in a single exercise—the formal test—when few if any of them will ever encounter a similar instrument once they have left school" (Gardner, 1993, pp. 175–176).

Gardner points out that, unlike tests, assessments are "intelligence fair." Most tests focus exclusively on linguistic and logical mathematical intelligences. If youngsters have strengths in these "intelligences" they will test well. If they do not have strengths in these areas they will not test well. Assessments can be engineered to address other intelligences, making assessments intelligence fair. For example, "Spatial intelligence can be assessed by having an individual navigate around an unfamiliar territory; bodily intelligence by seeing how a person learns and remembers a new dance or physical exercise; interpersonal intelligence by watching an individual handle a dispute with a salesclerk or navigate a way through a difficult committee meeting" (p. 176).

Gardner argues that assessment is far more sensitive to individual differences, developmental levels, and many forms of expertise. It allows for use of more intrinsically interesting materials and can be applied more directly for the student's benefit. Tests are sort of like baseball box scores. Box scores provide the data in runs, hits, and errors inning by inning. An assessment approach provides more vivid ways to communicate the drama and excitement of the game itself. Both approaches have a role to play. We know how to write up a box score but are just beginning to learn how to provide more vivid and meaningful portrayals of what has been learned and how to communicate this information to various audiences. If we want to be responsive to what parents, teachers, and students want and need, we will have to give more attention to assessments.

The Crow Island School in Winnetka, Illinois, does not emphasize box scores. Instead it provides a more detailed story of learning for each child. Twelve years ago the faculty at Crow Island designed a "Learning Experiences Form," which is illustrated in Figure 6.1.

Figure 6.1. Learning Experiences Form.

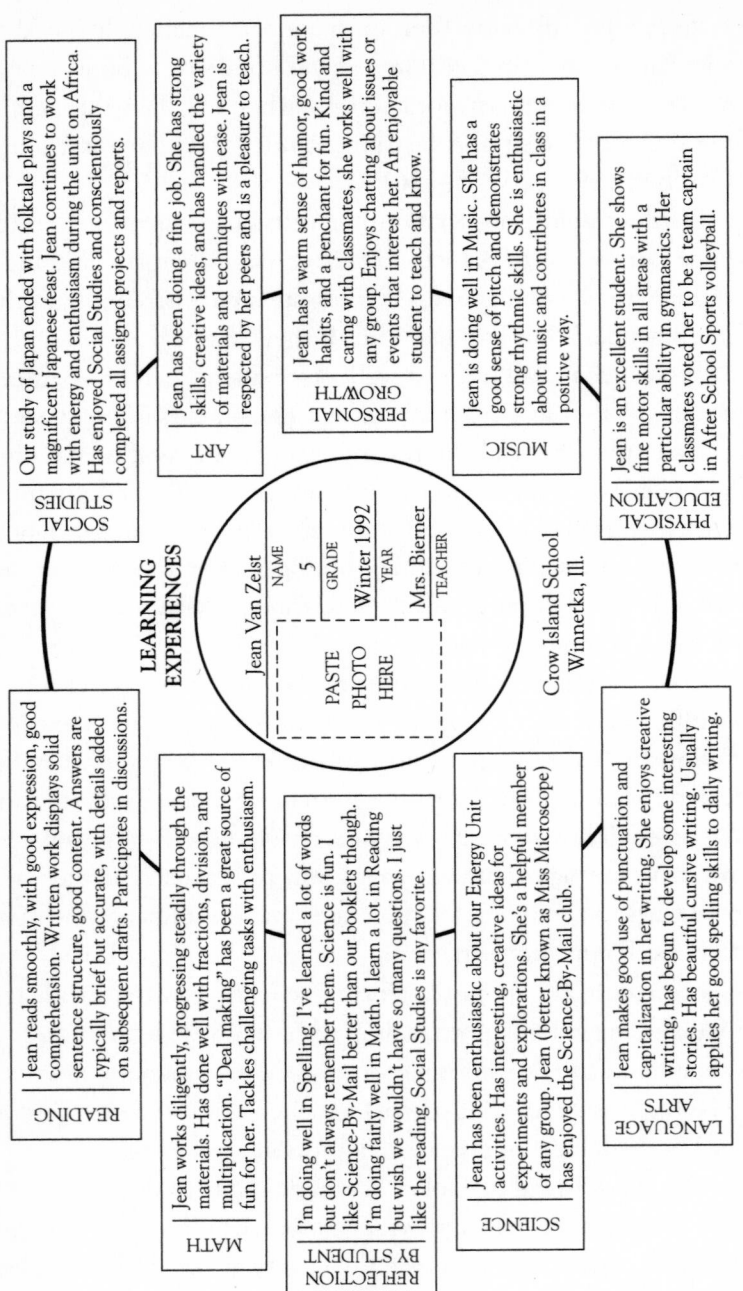

LEARNING EXPERIENCES

Jean Van Zelst

	NAME
PASTE	5
PHOTO	GRADE
HERE	Winter 1992
	YEAR
	Mrs. Biemer
	TEACHER

Crow Island School
Winnetka, Ill.

SOCIAL STUDIES
Our study of Japan ended with folktale plays and a magnificent Japanese feast. Jean continues to work with energy and enthusiasm during the unit on Africa. Has enjoyed Social Studies and conscientiously completed all assigned projects and reports.

ART
Jean has been doing a fine job. She has strong skills, creative ideas, and has handled the variety of materials and techniques with ease. Jean is respected by her peers and is a pleasure to teach.

PERSONAL GROWTH
Jean has a warm sense of humor, good work habits, and a penchant for fun. Kind and caring with classmates, she works well with any group. Enjoys chatting about issues or events that interest her. An enjoyable student to teach and know.

MUSIC
Jean is doing well in Music. She has a good sense of pitch and demonstrates strong rhythmic skills. She is enthusiastic about music and contributes in class in a positive way.

PHYSICAL EDUCATION
Jean is an excellent student. She shows fine motor skills in all areas with a particular ability in gymnastics. Her classmates voted her to be a team captain in After School Sports volleyball.

READING
Jean reads smoothly, with good expression, good comprehension. Written work displays solid sentence structure, good content. Answers are typically brief but accurate, with details added on subsequent drafts. Participates in discussions.

MATH
Jean works diligently, progressing steadily through the materials. Has done well with fractions, division, and multiplication. "Deal making" has been a great source of fun for her. Tackles challenging tasks with enthusiasm.

PERSONAL REFLECTION BY STUDENT
I'm doing well in Spelling. I've learned a lot of words but don't always remember them. Science is fun. I like Science-By-Mail better than our booklets though. I'm doing fairly well in Math. I learn a lot in Reading but wish we wouldn't have so many questions. I just like the reading. Social Studies is my favorite.

SCIENCE
Jean has been enthusiastic about our Energy Unit activities. Has interesting, creative ideas for experiments and explorations. She's a helpful member of any group. Jean (better known as Miss Microscope) has enjoyed the Science-By-Mail club.

LANGUAGE ARTS
Jean makes good use of punctuation and capitalization in her writing. She enjoys creative writing, has begun to develop some interesting stories. Has beautiful cursive writing. Usually applies her good spelling skills to daily writing.

Source: Hebert, 1992, p. 60.

Note that this form addresses each of the various intelligences proposed by Gardner and includes an opportunity for the student to reflect on his or her own personal progress. The development of this form launched a schoolwide conversation about assessment that continues to this day. Although the form itself has undergone many permutations over the years, the commitment to teaching children how to participate in the assessment of their own learning remains unchanged. All students maintain portfolios that they share with their parents each year at a child-led conference.

In seeking a progress report for your child or grandchild, which format would you prefer—a list of seven numbers indicating grades in the various subject matter areas or a series of learning experience forms combined with parent, teacher, and student conferences in which students share their portfolios and describe what they have learned and at what level? This is a tough question because both forms of reporting student progress can be useful. As pointed out in Chapter Five, I believe it is possible to craft a layered system of standards and shared accountability that provides both.

What we want are good schools. We want to be able to identify them, learn from them, and increase their number. These are the words used to introduce this chapter. They spell out a simple goal that few will disagree with and a difficult task that many puzzle over. We do not always agree on what a good school is. In our multicultural society with multiple layers of governance and accountability we have different interests and different stakes in our educational system. These interests and stakes shade our view of what is good. The fact is that corporations, state governments, parents, teachers, students, the local police department, welfare administration officials, and others just don't see eye to eye on all school issues.

Yet at a broad level, I think we can agree that good schools share some commonalities even though they are different. Good schools are good for two reasons: because they measure up to these commonalities and because they can respond to their unique local context, constituents, purposes, visions, and circumstances.

Thanks to the contributions of such experts as Wiggins (1993, 1996), Tucker and Codding (1997), Darling-Hammond and Falk (1997), Marzano and Kendall (1996), and many others, we have amassed solid knowledge about standards and assessments that can help us with our work. But to take full advantage of what we know, we need to bring together the interests of parents, teachers, students, local citizens, the state, the business community, and other stakeholders into a coherent layered system that combines high standards with carefully thought out and useful assessments.

The Quality Review Process

One possibility worth exploring is to borrow from the experiences of New York and Illinois with the school quality review process. These states have constructed a system of standards and assessments that rely not only on standardized tests but also on a variety of other assessments. The school quality review process was a concept imported to the United States by Thomas Sobol in 1992 when he was New York State Commissioner of Education. With the help of David Green (1995; Ancess, 1996), who served for ten years as one of Her Majesty's Inspectors of Schools in England, the U.K. approach has undergone adjustments in both New York and Illinois designed to make it more democratic and responsive to local needs.

With Sobol's departure as commissioner, the review process has received less attention in New York but has since been implemented in Illinois. The process requires the putting together of a team of state and local representatives, parents, teachers, students, and others who make three to five daylong visits to a school and engage in a holistic and in-depth assessment of what is going on. Team members may visit classrooms, attend faculty meetings, examine student work, review documents, interview students, teachers, and parents, and engage in other activities. Of particular interest are any school improvement plans that the local school has and the extent to which those plans are being implemented. The review process requires a direct examination of practice, an analysis of self-review information, and the preparation of a report. Both the school's own goals and external standards are used in reviewing the school and in providing information.

Ancess (1996) notes that five principles are key to the review process: "(1) responsiveness to the culture of the school, (2) reliance on the team's collective perspective to safeguard against subjectivity, (3) development of building-level capacity, (4) stimulation of inquiry, and (5) support for professionalism" (p. 5). The school's own goals, sense of mission, values, and beliefs, and not those of reviewers, drive the review process. No template from the outside is brought in to assess the extent to which a school measures up. "Reviewers strive to get to know the school on its own ground, and in a context of respect and support" (Ancess, 1996, p. 5).

Further, it is assumed that schools can make a difference by taking responsibility for building their own capacity to function more effectively. Review teams function as critical friends who raise questions about contradictions between stated intents and observed practices. "Working against the grain of most packaged professional development programs and prescriptions, a team's questions may leave a school community temporarily puzzled and frustrated, for they must unpack the questions in order to derive direction from them. When a school adopts a team's questions as a starting point for its inquiry, however, it can enter into a process of individual and collective reflection. The culture of inquiry that this can fuel can keep a school focused on its quest to achieve its goals" (Ancess, 1996, p. 7).

According to Illinois accountability and assurance guidelines (Illinois State Board of Education, 1997–1998), "Any school review process, whether internal or external, must assure that all stakeholders are able to contribute to the crafting of this process. It should affirm the critical importance of teaching and engage them in a discussion and review of teaching and learning. Schools should be afforded sufficient flexibility to represent their work in a manner they deem appropriate, both to their fellow professionals and to members of the wider community" (p. 2). Further, "The Quality Review and Improvement Planning program will place great emphasis on supporting schools, and less on accumulating documentation; it will help to promote effective school inquiry and useful school improvement planning. It will be developed on a school by school basis, recognizing the different circumstances of schools, and linking school improvement to accountability" (p. 3).

Illinois uses a three-pronged approach to its review: school improvement planning at the school site that includes the school's vision, goals, and targets and the strategies needed to achieve them; an internal review in the form of a rigorous self-analysis, involving parents, school community members, and educators that focuses on the school's policies and practices, goals and objectives, and the extent to which they are being met; and an external review conducted by a visiting team of educators, parents, and state officials that are not affiliated with either the school or the school district.

> The most important aspect of planning is a school staff's rigorous consideration of certain basic questions: (1) Are all students learning? (2) How do we know they are learning? (3) What changes need to be made in our program so that all students will be successful? Corollaries to these questions are (1) Where are we? (2) Where do we want to go? and (3) How will we get there?
>
> Internal and External reviews focus on three areas: (1) Teaching and Learning; (2) Student Learning, Progress, and Achievement; and (3) the Learning Community. In each of these areas, specific topics are reviewed through direct observations in classrooms; shadowing students; interviewing teachers, parents, staff, and others; studying documents such as the School Improvement Plan; analyzing assessment results; and examining various artifacts of student work such as portfolios, sci-

ence projects, and works of art [Illinois State Board of Education, 1998, p. 3].

What distinguishes the school review process described here from the usual way we handle accountability in the United States is that the basic requirements for planning and the indicators of effectiveness are not provided as detailed prescriptions by the state. Illinois does provide frameworks to guide the work of local schools, but frameworks are not the same as planning models. "A model is a representation of something with specific patterns and typical forms. In school improvement planning, a model is a detailed and concrete set of plans that is a replication (or at least a partial replication) of other improvement plans that are quite similar. A planning model provides specific directions for critical choices which school planners must take. A framework provides direction; a model provides directions" (Illinois State Board of Education, 1998, pp. 6–7).

While taking into account standardized test scores, both internal and external review teams emphasize local standards and goals, grades that students earn, and actual work that they do. Thus displays of student work in halls and classrooms, portfolios of student work, oral presentations, homework samples, daily classroom work, work derived from community service projects, and learning that comes from before-school and after-school activities are also rigorously examined and taken into account in assessing a school. The Illinois quality review process "encourages schools to build on their previous work in this area, and provides flexibility in the continued development of assessment systems to ensure that they support a school's mission, curriculum, and instruction. Review teams, therefore, review how a school assesses student progress, and how the school determines which procedures contribute to the overall assessment system" (Illinois State Board of Education, 1997–1998, p. 12).

An outline of an internal or external review includes attention to the following categories of information:

1. Teaching and Learning

   Learning environment

   Instructional strategies

   Learning processes

   Student responses

2. Student Learning, Progress, and Achievement

   Curriculum design and alignment

   Student work

   Assessment systems

3. The Learning Community

   Mission and shared vision

   Leadership and administration

   Organizational structure

   Professional development and support for staff

   Community participation in the school-based learning community

Examples of text from external review reports appear as Appendices A and B.

One important advantage of the school quality review process is that it permits review teams to provide a context for student achievement results relative to both state-mandated and locally determined standards. One set of standards applied in the same way to all students creates problems for those students who are not prepared to reach them. Wolk (1998) points out, for example, that many high school and middle school students do not read well enough to pass tests based on these decontextualized standards. In his words:

> For tens of thousands of urban youngsters, it's a kind of double jeopardy: the system failed to educate them ade-

quately and now it punishes them for not being edu-
cated. These kids have not been exposed to the high
standards, highly trained teachers, and rich curriculum
that the standards-based reform promises—and must
deliver if it is to succeed. Some states are determined to
hold students accountable even though most teachers
haven't been prepared to teach to high standards and
won't be for years to come [p. 48].

Within the school quality review process, however, the context
for teaching and learning is discussed and assessed. If, for example,
teachers are not prepared well enough to teach a specific subject to
a high standard, then the report focuses on that problem rather than
dwelling on student achievement rates and test scores.

Process Counts Too

The world-renowned management expert W. Edwards Deming
taught that separating goals, targets, and other outcome measures
from the processes needed to accomplish them is useless. To him,
emphasizing process is at least as important, and may even be more
important, as emphasizing results. In his words, "You can beat
horses; they run faster for awhile. Goals are like hay somebody ties
in front of the horse's snout. The horse is smart enough to discover
no matter whether he canters or gallops, trots or walks or stands
still, he can't catch up with the hay. Might as well stand still. Why
argue about it? It will not happen except by change of the system.
That's management's job, not the people's" (quoted in Walton,
1986, p. 77).

Deming's words remind us that a good quality review is based on
both processes and substance, on both how things are done and
what is accomplished, on both school climate factors and on student learning standards and achievements. While focusing on
results alone may be misguided, focusing on purposes alone may

result in a weak review. This is why locally developed and rigorous standards for learning, written by parents, teachers, and students, must be at the heart and soul of the quality review process.

As suggested in Chapter Five, if locals connected to a particular school are not comfortable with or able to develop learning standards alone, they should receive assistance from local school districts or state experts. Locals should also be able to consult standards banks (lists of standards retrievable on the Internet or in some other way). These standards banks could be made available by the state, by the various subject-matter specialty groups (for example, National Council of Teachers of English), or by other groups (Council for Basic Education, Center on Learning, Assessment, and School Structure, National Center on Education and the Economy). Some standards might be adopted for local use "as is" and others might be used to help frame the writing of local standards.

States have an important responsibility in this process. Their job is to develop standards for standards and to use them to ensure that local standards are legitimate. Thus, while local standards will differ, some assurance that local standards are of good quality will exist. Once schools have locally determined the standards for each of the subject matter areas taught, these standards should help guide the quality review process.

Who Should Be Responsible for What

In Table 6.1, I provide an overview of what might be one way to distribute responsibility among various stakeholders for setting standards and for assessing schools. I propose that there might be standards in five areas:

- Standards for all schools in basic reading, writing, and math

- Focused and varied standards in key curriculum areas such as history, advanced math, English, art, music, and social sciences

- Focused and varied standards in social and emotional learning areas including character development

- School standards in noncurriculum areas such as teacher development, use of resources, and sense of community

- Teacher standards in such areas as professionalism, collegiality, and professional growth

To begin the conversation, I propose that the state assume 90 percent of the responsibility for setting standards in the basic skills areas and that these areas be tested by standardized tests. For the focused and varied standards in the key curriculum areas, I propose that the state assume 15 percent of the responsibility and the local school and its school district 85 percent of the responsibility. I have in mind something like 60 percent of the responsibility allocated to the individual school and 25 percent of the responsibility allocated to the district. For the focused and varied standards in social and emotional learning, I propose a 40-60 split between state and local authorities. With respect to school standards in noncurriculum areas, the state might assume 40 percent of the responsibility for setting standards and the local school and district 60 percent. With respect to teachers' standards, the state might assume 60 percent of the responsibility and the local school and school district 40 percent of the responsibility. If the state sets up an independent professional teaching board to oversee teaching standards, then that board would play the major role. Such a board would presumably be heavily staffed by teachers and representatives of teacher organizations.

Although standardized tests would dominate in assessing basic reading, math, and writing, they would play a much less important role for focused and varied standards in key curriculum areas, a negligible role for focused and varied standards in social and emotional areas, and no role in assessing school standards and teacher standards. In these areas the dominant assessment vehicle would be the whole school quality review process, involving both an internal self-study

Table 6.1. Layered Standards, Shared Accountability.

Standards	Standardized standards in basic reading, math, and writing	Focused and varied standards in key curriculum areas such as history, advanced math, literature, art, and social science	Focused and varied standards in social and emotional learning areas, including character development	School standards in noncurriculum areas such as teacher development, use of resources, and sense of community	Teacher standards in such areas as professionalism, collegiality, professional growth, and quality of practice
Responsibility for setting	State 90% Local 10%	State 15% Local 85%	State 40% Local 60%	State 40% Local 60%	State 60% * Local 40%
Primary assessment strategies	Standardized tests	Tests, portfolios, performance exhibitions, internal review self-study, observation, interview	Portfolios, performance exhibitions, service requirement, internal review self-study, observation, interview	State indicator system, local self-study	State indicator system, local self-study
Responsibility for assessment	State with results considered by WSQR team	WSQR team that includes state and local representatives, parents, teachers, students, local citizens	WSQR team	WSQR team	WSQR team
Product	One report that provides an in-depth study of the school and a summary rating that takes into account all layers of standards and their assessment				
Audience for report	In order of importance: the local school, the school community, the school district, the state, the general public				

Note: WSQR = Whole School Quality Review

* If the state sets up an independent professional teaching board, the distribution will be different, with the board playing the major role.

review and a visitation team that would engage in an intensive examination of each individual school. In the social and emotional learning areas, performance exhibitions, portfolios, and perhaps a service requirement would make sense. With respect to school standards in noncurriculum areas, it might make sense for the state to develop some sort of indicator system that the local school quality review team would consider along with local self-study data. A similar approach might work for teacher standards, again assuming there is no independent state teacher standards board.

Who would be responsible for assessing? The state would be responsible for assessing standards in basic reading, math, and writing, and its findings would have to be considered by the whole school quality review team. The whole school quality review team would be the major player in all other assessments. This team would develop one report that provides an in-depth study of the school and a summary rating that takes into account all layers of standards and their assessment. In other words, if a state chooses to sort schools into categories such as exemplary, recognized, meets expectations, and needs improvement, *no one source of data can be used alone in reaching this summative evaluation*. In order of importance the audience for the report would be the local school, the local school community, the school district, the state, and the general public.

Will a system of whole school quality review work? I don't know. But I think it has potential. What are the obstacles to creating a school quality review system that incorporates layered standards and shared accountability? Certainly it is not a lack of talent. We already know how to assess with a high level of sophistication, and we know that the concept of layered loyalties makes sense. It is, after all, a part of the everyday lives of most Americans who believe in their country, their church, their lodge, their ethnic background, their politics, their local community, their family, and even their local schools all at the same time. Somehow all these layers of loyalties are held together by certain common characteristics that define us as Americans. Similarly, schools, like neighborhoods within a city, would be tied together by some common standards but would celebrate their diversity and their uniqueness by being connected to different standards at the same time.

Alfred North Whitehead said in his book *Symbolism, Its Meaning and Effect* (1927):

> It is the first step in sociological wisdom, to recognize that the major advances in civilization are processes which all but wreck the societies in which they occur:— like unto an arrow in the hand of a child. The art of free society consists first in the maintenance of the symbolic code; and secondly in fearlessness of revision, to secure that the code serves those purposes which satisfy an enlightened reason. Those societies which cannot combine reverence to their symbols with freedom of revision, must ultimately decay either from anarchy, or from the slow atrophy of a life stifled by useless shadows [p. 88].

If talent is not an obstacle and disposition is not an obstacle, what is? Will! Do we have the will to take a course that departs dramatically from our comfortable and accustomed "one best way" approach to things? Are we ready, in other words, for that proverbial paradigm change with respect to standards and assessment? When it comes to change we are, after all, a conservative lot. That conservatism can be a virtue when it is balanced with a certain flexibility that allows us to move ahead in light of new conditions.

Teachers: Keys to School Improvement

This chapter's theme is teachers, their work, and their learning. It is based on a simple premise. The more teachers know and the more skilled they are in teaching, the more successful schools will be in advancing learning. Whether teachers will know more and become more skilled depends upon the support they get from policies and contexts (see the National Commission on Teaching and America's Future, 1996). In many places teaching is undervalued, and the conditions for supporting teachers are underdeveloped. This situation has consequences for the lifeworld of teachers and schools.

Supporting Teaching

The lifeworld is concerned with cultural things, and the systemsworld is concerned with instrumental things. Lifeworlds are very important in schools and other social organizations such as families, churches, friendship networks, and mutual help associations. But lifeworlds alone are not sufficient. The systemsworld provides the means to help achieve and embody cultural goals. In Chapter Two we noted that both individual and school character counts. We reviewed evidence that school character and school effectiveness are linked. A rule of thumb is that school character grows when lifeworld requirements determine systemsworld decisions. And school character erodes when systemsworld requirements determine life-world decisions. When this happens local discretion over ends is reduced. Schools begin to look alike. Teachers start to teach the same things in the same ways to all students. Instead of form following function, function begins to follow form.

Where do teachers fit into this picture? Right in the middle. Teachers ultimately determine whether a school will be an effective one. But not everyone agrees that well-trained teachers are that important. In the United States, as compared with most other developed countries, we have underinvested in teaching and have overinvested in the management of teaching.

The National Commission on Teaching and America's Future (1996) notes, for example, that "although more and more adults are working in schools, fewer and fewer are actually in the classroom. Indeed, the proportion of professional staff classified as teachers has declined consistently over the years, from more than 70 percent in 1950 to 52 percent in 1993. Of these more than 10 percent are specialists not engaged in classroom teaching" (pp. 47–48). According to the National Center for Educational Statistics, though the ratio of total staff to pupils in the United States is 1:9, the ratio of teaching staff to pupils is 1:18 (Darling-Hammond, 1997, p. 192). Using data from the Organization for Economic Cooperation and Development, the National Commission (1996) reports that while teachers in France, Finland, Australia, Italy, Japan, and Belgium represent, on average, 70 percent of the educational staff, teachers in the United States represent only 43 percent of the educational staff (p. 70).

By and large most developed countries invest more than the United States does in teacher preparation, teacher professional development, and teacher planning. Darling-Hammond (1996) points out that teachers in the United States have only three to five hours a week available for planning, leaving them precious little time for consulting with colleagues or learning about new teaching strategies. Many of their European and Asian counterparts, by contrast, spend between fifteen and twenty hours a week working together on refining lessons and learning new techniques.

Strategies for Managing Teaching and Learning

Different views of teaching and different estimates of the importance of having highly qualified teachers in every classroom lead states and countries to choose different strategies for managing teaching and learning. States and countries can rely on only one strategy or a combination of six different strategies: direct supervision of teachers, standardizing the work that teachers do, standardizing the outcomes that teachers are expected to achieve, professionalizing teaching, linking teachers morally to shared purposes and ideals, and providing newer forms of collegiality that lead to the development of communities of practice among teachers (Mintzberg, 1979; Sergiovanni, 1992). The choices that states and countries make are directly related to two things: the extent to which policymakers value teachers and believe teachers are capable of practicing as professionals; and the views of policymakers about the nature of teaching expertise.

When states, for example, rely on direct supervision, principals and other supervisors are expected to provide teachers with clear directions as to what should be done and how it should be done. They are then expected to follow up personally by engaging in close supervision. When states rely on standardizing the work that teachers do, emphasis shifts from personal inspection to impersonal control by providing a "one best way" system in the form of an explicitly detailed curriculum. This curriculum comes complete with lesson plans, time frames, and tests that teachers are required to use. Completing the picture are management strategies to ensure that the work of teachers is properly aligned and timetables are followed and that teaching and curriculum scripts are used.

Both direct supervision of teachers and standardization of the work of teachers are highly visible and heavy-handed approaches to managing teaching that are not as popular as they once were. Most reformers agree, for example, that teachers need to be free to make decisions within certain standardized and specified boundaries. This view gives rise to the third strategy—providing standards and outcomes as a form of control. This strategy ensures that every student in the state will produce similar products, learn the same things, and reach the same levels of performance. The touted advantage of this strategy is that teachers are able to have a measure of control over the means by deciding how they will achieve the required standards. But as has been previously argued, this strategy winds up scripting what people do. Standards require uniform assessments; these assessments become the curriculum, and this curriculum dictates the teaching. Teacher discretion is diluted as a result.

Together the three strategies share a certain distrust of teachers— a lack of faith in their capacity to make good decisions and a lack of trust in their willingness to work hard on behalf of their students. There may be reasons for this lack of faith and trust. As long as we rely on management strategies that remove discretion, teaching will not develop properly into a profession worthy of faith and trust.

Changing Our Strategies

Changing this situation requires changing our strategies. Let's consider, for example, the merits of strategies that promote capacity building and the development of professional norms. Capacity building and professional norms increase what teachers know, are able to do, and are willing to do to help students learn. These strategies include professional socialization and development; involving teachers in establishing shared purposes, values, and norms that provide frames and standards for their practice; and creating opportunities for heightened collegiality that leads to greater interdependence among teachers and to the development of communities of practice.

Changing teaching into a profession worthy of faith and trust requires changing the views of policymakers. It is commonly believed, for example, that teaching is easy to learn and do. Teaching involves identifying and using certain skills that can be readily acquired, monitored, and assessed. Because of this attitude, policymakers believe it is less important to invest in professionalism, collegiality, the development of communities of practice, and other expensive capacity-building strategies to improve schools. After all, as a visit to a McDonald's restaurant will reveal, simple work can be done well by most people if they are properly managed. So, we invest in direct supervision, standardizing teachers' work, and standardizing outcomes as a means to ensure that teaching measures up.

Understanding Professional Expertise

What is professional expertise in teaching really like? Mary Kennedy (1987) identifies several dimensions, three of which are as follows: (1) professional expertise is the accumulation and use of certain technical skills; (2) professional expertise is the development and application of conceptual knowledge, general principles, and theories; and (3) professional expertise is the ability to engage in deliberate action (p. 1). The accumulation of technical skills emphasizes the specific tasks that teachers must perform and the skills they must demonstrate to engage in these tasks successfully. Teachers need to plan lessons, organize work stations, redirect student behavior, use small groups, conduct Socratic seminars, discipline students, and so on.

As valuable as skills are to professional practice, skills alone provide a narrow and decontextualized view of teaching. Skills need to be accompanied by other dimensions so that teachers are able to decide which skills to use and why and when to use these skills. If professional expertise were defined only as the accumulation and use of skills, then teaching would be much less of a profession than it is and managing teaching by direct supervision and standardization of work and outcomes would be appropriate. Further, the decision to provide teachers with discretion or not would not be an issue. Discretion would not be high priority.

Professional expertise as the application of general principles provides teachers with knowledge that enables them to treat specific situations as examples of categories about which something is known. This knowledge enables them to solve problems, find solutions, and make decisions about what to do in ambiguous situations (Kennedy, 1987).

Professional expertise as deliberative action acknowledges that teaching practice is situated in a context that involves, for example, different resources, students, needs, time constraints, and curriculum frameworks. Teachers bring to this context different purposes, and the interaction between purposes and contexts shapes what they do. Teachers analyze different situations and monitor how situations change as practice unfolds, crafting strategies that combine action with thinking. One idea leads to another until a pattern emerges (Mintzberg, 1987, p. 68).

Once a pattern emerges teachers are able to use knowledge of general principles and their experiences together to make good decisions. This analysis occurs within the context of one's unique teaching practice. Donald Schön's (1983) research, for example, shows that expert professionals generate knowledge as they engage in the particulars of practice, spontaneously forming intuitions and discovering new paths they were not able to anticipate beforehand. They create their practice through use. Kennedy (1987) points out, "Successful deliberate action requires a body of experiences on which to draw, the ability to conduct mental experiments, the ability to evaluate their outcomes critically, and the ability to revise one's definition of the situation. . . . In addition, it requires a highly developed sense of purpose, for purpose is the criterion against which both ideas and action are judged" (pp. 29–30).

Wilson and Peterson (1997) argue that teachers are intellectuals who think about students and subject matter and construct bridges between the two. "Good teachers must think hard about what they want their students to learn, contemplating myriad questions. A teacher must consider questions like: What is interesting about this subject matter for my students? What ideas and concepts are particularly difficult? Why? What are the different means I can use to help students grapple with these ideas? What do my students already know that might help? What do they believe that might get in the way? What time of the day is it? The year? What resources do I have access to? How do students construct their understandings? What teaching moves can I make to help that process of meaning construction?" (pp. 8–9). Wilson and Peterson point out further that teachers are listeners and inquirers who research their practice by investigating students' thinking and searching for ways to teach for understanding. And finally, teachers are coaches who support students as they learn to demonstrate what they know.

The three dimensions of professional expertise, when appropriately applied to teaching, are nested. The acquisition and use of skills is embedded in and flows from the development and use of general principles. General principles, in turn, are embedded in and flow from deliberative action. Deliberative action, with its concept of teacher as intellectual artisan, encompasses the other two dimensions providing a challenging, yet realistic, view of teaching and learning. This view provides a sharp contrast with a "skills only" approach or even with a "skills plus general principles" approach, within which teachers master and apply a set of generalizations and regularities that are context free and thus thought to apply to all students, on all occasions, everywhere.

We began this discussion of professional expertise by pointing out that if teaching is simply the application of "one best way" skills, then discretion is not an issue, and teaching and learning is best managed by direct supervision and standardizing the work and outcomes. But if teaching is intellectual work, as described earlier, then these are the wrong strategies because they limit discretion.

Capacity-building strategies, such as emphasizing professional development and socialization, heightening levels of collegiality, and developing communities of practice, are more effective alternatives. They are investments in the long-term effectiveness of schools. Once established they become substitutes for strong emphasis on management systems and for externally imposed accountability designs.

Chapter Three acknowledged that teaching is founded on methods of teaching and mastery of various disciplines. But a complete definition of professionalism encompasses certain virtues, including that of making a public commitment to serve ideas and people. Caring is the cornerstone of this commitment and has an important role to play in developing a full understanding of professional expertise. Building on the discussion in Chapter Three, we now move to a consideration of teacher motivation and teacher efficacy and how they are related to student achievement. The view of teachers as interdependent artisans who are members of communities of practice will also be examined.

Motivation, Efficacy, and Student Performance

The lifeworlds of teachers are fragile. When motivation is down and discretion is low, a teacher's sense of self-esteem becomes blurred. The lifeworlds of teachers can easily erode as a result. Ultimately efficacy is affected. When this happens, teachers feel that they do not count. Teacher efficacy is directly related to how teachers behave in the classroom, to students' behavior in the classroom, and to the quality of student achievement teachers obtain. Teacher efficacy is an important factor in building an effective school.

Let's begin by examining teacher efficacy and its effects on student achievement, paying particular attention to the conditions of teaching and schooling that either enhance or diminish this efficacy. Rather than reviewing the broad literature on this topic (see Bandura, 1977, 1982) we will focus on one particularly important study conducted by Patricia Ashton and Rodmann Webb (1986).

"All students can learn" has become a common slogan that is repeated by administrators to urge teachers to work harder or to change their practices. It appears in book after book on schooling and in the mission and vision statements of thousands of schools across the globe. Virtually every teacher will swear allegiance to this slogan publicly, but privately not everyone believes it. Ashton and Webb (1986) found that teachers with a low sense of efficacy had come to believe that many students cannot learn and will not learn and that there isn't much a teacher can do about it. This is just a reality that has to be accepted. Teachers with a high sense of efficacy, on the other hand, believe that all students are capable of learning—that teachers can do a great deal to increase student achievement.

These differences are important. Put a modern school plant, terrific books, and a well-thought-out curriculum in the hands of the first group of teachers, and students will not learn much. Restructuring the schools by creating larger blocks of time, adding an advisory, and dividing the school into smaller learning academies might be helpful, but still students will not learn very much if teachers do not believe that students are able to learn.

Ashton and Webb noted that there is a second dimension to a teacher's sense of efficacy. Not only does it refer to the belief that students can learn if taught but to a teacher's belief that she or he has the ability to do the right kind of teaching that will result in student learning.

Defining teachers' sense of efficacy as a belief that students can learn if taught and as a belief in one's own ability to successfully teach them, Ashton and Webb found that teachers with a high sense of efficacy exhibited warmth. They were more accepting of student responses and initiatives and more attentive to student needs. Students responded by being more enthusiastic and by initiating more interactions with the teachers. Further, student achievement was higher in tests of both high school mathematics and basic language skills.

Enhancing Efficacy

The good news is that teachers' sense of efficacy can change. Teachers can come to feel more or less efficacious depending on a variety of factors. Further, higher levels of motivation and commitment and higher levels of efficacy seem related to each other. What are the factors that contribute to these higher levels? Ashton and Webb found that school climates that are supportive, teaching and learning environments that are characterized by collegial values and shared decision making, and school cultures that provide a sense of purpose and a shared covenant as a basis for accountability are important. Together these factors contribute to cooperative relationships, higher levels of interaction, higher levels of personal responsibility for outcomes, and higher standards and expectations, as well as a sense that the work of teaching is meaningful and significant. These relationships are summarized in Figure 7.1.

In summary, efficacy is important. Individual efficacy is an important part of the lifeworlds of teachers, and collective efficacy is an important part of the lifeworlds of schools. Both suffer when bureaucratic policies, management systems, and mandated "one size fits all" standards and assessments determine the cultural worlds of teachers and other locals.

At root, *efficacy* means having the power to produce a desired effect. In schools power strengthens both purposes and people when it is linked to shared purposes, values, and beliefs that define lifeworlds. For power to have this effect, a top-down or externally imposed pyramid image of authority needs to be exchanged for a circle image as shown in Figure 7.2. Within the circle image, principals, teachers, parents, students, and other locals are empowered and enabled to meet their commitments to ideas that they value, share, and accept.

Trading the triangle for the circle provides a democratic culture that functions as a powerful force for change at the local level. Lavuan Dennett, recalling her experiences as principal of an elementary school that made dramatic improvements in student performance,

Figure 7.1. Factors Contributing to Teachers' Sense of Efficacy, Motivation, and Commitment.

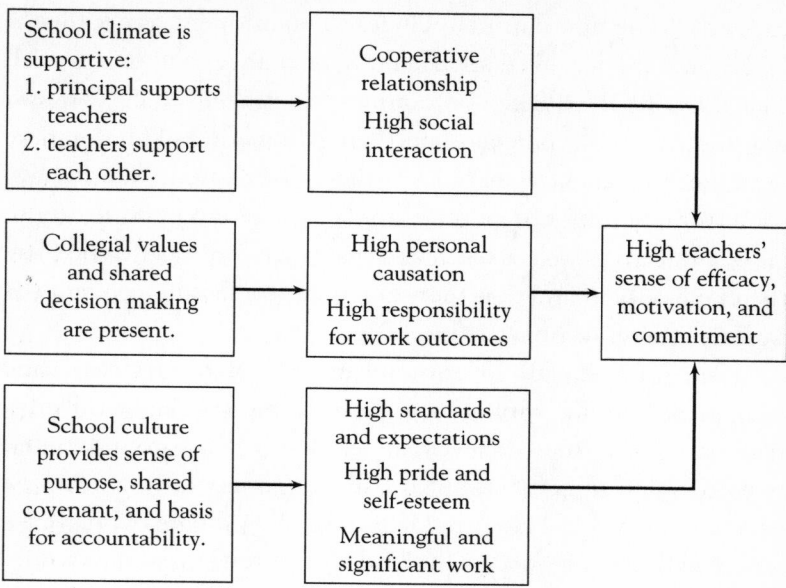

Source: Adapted from Sergiovanni, 1990, p. 131.

Figure 7.2. A Community View of Power.

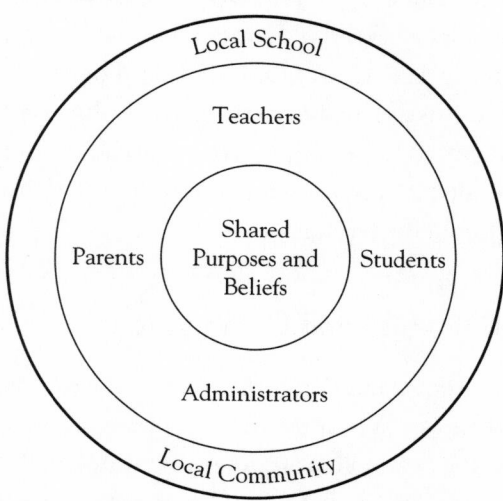

Source: Adapted from Sergiovanni, 1990, p. 105.

explains, "The new culture includes a commitment to excellence and an acceptance, even appreciation, of change that assures us all that this school will keep becoming what it needs to be. We lead one another in this process of becoming. Sometimes I fill that role, sometimes a teacher, sometimes a student or a parent. We all have something of importance to share. We all get an opportunity to grow and learn as well as teach and share. We continue to complete the circle only to find that there are more wonderful opportunities waiting" (Sergiovanni, 1990, p. 105).

Many state officials, superintendents, corporate executives, and even principals are wary of suggestions that power be broadly distributed. "Look, there is just so much power to go around. Sure I need to share some of it, but if I share too much, how can I be expected to lead? If I don't hold on to the lion's share of power the school will just not work." This kind of reasoning makes sense if we view power from the perspective of economics. There is a fixed sum of power available that represents 100 percent. If I give 20 percent of it away, I will have 80 percent left. If I give 60 percent away I will have only 40 percent left. But research on power in organizations suggests that power actually expands as it is shared. Sharing power is a form of investment that provides more power for everyone in the end. The work of Arnold Tannenbaum on this topic, summarized in Exhibit 7.1, is considered seminal. His work leads to the conclusion that it is not so much strong leadership from the top but the total amount of leadership exercised in a school that counts. Leadership density, it appears, is an undervalued and underused contributor to school effectiveness.

Teacher Motivation and Commitment

Efficacy, motivation, and commitment are linked together and to school effectiveness. When parents, teachers, students, and other locals believe they can make an important difference in improving their schools they are likely to be more motivated and committed

Exhibit 7.1. Power: Investing in Capacity Building.

The research literature on power in organizations provides strong support for directing enabling leadership to empowering the school site. The work of University of Michigan professor Arnold Tannenbaum is considered seminal. He found that leaders can actually increase control by giving up authority. Furthermore, power and influence should not be considered as zero-sum economic concepts. Sharing power means more power for everyone—power has the capacity to expand.

Tannenbaum found that the total amount of power and influence that existed in an enterprise across ranks was a better predictor of satisfaction and performance than was the relative amount of power and influence held by any one group as compared with another. His ideas apply as well to schools. Imagine, for example, two schools with influence patterns on a one-to-ten scale as follows:

School A		School B	
Parents	2	Parents	4
Teachers	3	Teachers	6
Principal	4	Principal	9
Sum	9	Sum	19

In School A power is fairly "equally" shared among parents, teachers and principals with a difference of one noted for teachers as compared with principals and parents as compared with teachers. In School B, the differences are three and two, thus power is distributed in a somewhat less "equal" manner. The sum of power in School A, however, is less than one-half of that for School B. Tannenbaum would predict that though the distribution within School B is less equal, B would report higher levels of satisfaction and higher levels of performance across the board. The reasoning being that school site B was more empowered than A.

Source: Sergiovanni, 1990.

to act. We have reviewed some of the research on efficacy, but what about motivation and commitment?

In successful schools, teachers work harder, are more satisfied with their jobs, and are committed to the school and its work. These motivating conditions are present when teachers and others

- Find their work lives to be meaningful, purposeful, sensible, and significant, and when they view the work itself as worthwhile and important.

- Have reasonable control over their work activities and affairs and are able to exert reasonable influence over work events and circumstances.

- Experience personal responsibility for the work and are personally responsible for outcomes. (See Chapter 10 in Sergiovanni, 1995, for an elaboration of these ideas.)

Teachers are more likely to experience meaningfulness, control, and personal responsibility when they are allowed to function as "Origins" rather than as "Pawns." According to De Charms (1968), "An Origin is a person who perceives his behavior as determined by his own choosing. A Pawn is a person who perceives his behavior as determined by external forces beyond his control." De Charms continues: "An Origin has a strong feeling of personal causation, a feeling that the locus for causation of effects in his environment lies within himself . . . a Pawn has a feeling that causal forces beyond his control, or personal forces residing within others, or in the physical environment determine his behavior. This constitutes a strong feeling of powerlessness or ineffectiveness" (p. 274). In referring to Pawn feelings and behavior among teachers the economist and Nobel laureate Theodore Schultz (1982) states, "Most of these attitudes of school teachers should have been anticipated in view of the way schools are organized and administered. The curriculum is not for them to decide; nor is the content of the course to be taught and the plans to be followed. . . . School teachers are responding to the much circumscribed opportunities open to them. They are not robots but human agents who perceive, interpret, and act in accordance with the worthwhile options available" (p. 43). Perhaps the issue can be framed this way. If you view teaching as simple work that requires the following of rules, the teaching of scripts, and the following of bureaucratic mandates, then the more pawn-like teaching behavior is, the better. That way we can be sure that teachers will do what they are supposed to.

If, however, you believe the work of teaching to be complex, then a more professional stance makes sense. Bureaucrats, for example, are subordinate to the knowledge base of teaching. Professionals, on the other hand, are superordinate to this knowledge base. For them knowledge does not tell them what to do but informs their intuitions so that they are able to make better decisions about their practice. "Responsive to unique situations, professionals take their cues from the problems they face and the students they serve. They draw on the wealth of knowledge and technology available to them as they create professional knowledge in use in response to student needs. Bureaucrats, by contrast, are not driven by student problems but by the technology itself. They are appliers of rules, regulators of formats, direction followers, and managerial implementers. They strive for a 'one best way' to treat all cases, and, pursuing standard outcomes, they apply formal procedures in standardized ways. It is in this sense that legislated learning and bureaucratic teaching encourages Pawn feelings and behaviors among teachers and students, contributing to less effective teaching and learning" (Sergiovanni, 1995, p. 253).

The Artisan Metaphor

Teachers are often viewed as independent artisans who use well-honed skills anchored to theories and principles. They acknowledge the contextualized nature of teaching practice by using deliberative action. They make responsive decisions that allow for the creation of their practice in use (Kennedy, 1987; Wilson and Peterson, 1997). The artisan metaphor for teaching highlights the importance of discretion. To function as independent artisans teachers need to be autonomous enough to use the expertise needed to make on-the-spot decisions, to solve problems, to invent practices, and to think about and understand what they are doing. But, as Huberman (1988) points out, the independent artisan metaphor has serious limitations:

- Main sources of professional self-esteem, competence, and outside expertise are either private . . . or external to the [school] building.

- The interdependencies between artisans of different trades [teachers who teach different subjects or at different grade levels] working in the same building are weak ones and have to do mostly with getting the right conditions for satisfying customers. Only in extreme cases does something happening in one . . . [classroom] affect what an artisan does in another.

- There are some powerful norms floating around . . . that each artisan is autonomous, and cooperates only when she chooses to.

- Only artisans of the same guild [members of the same department or grade level] with a similar approach can offer meaningful professional advice.

- The status or prestige of each artisan in the building is equal.

- Artisans in the building do not inspect one another's work.

- One [artisan] intrudes sparingly on the time and energy of others in the building so as not to distract them from what each considers to be her core functions, the ones carried out in [their own classrooms] [p. 3].

Huberman's image of independent artisans is that of teachers who practice their craft privately and who interact sparingly with only a select few artisans of the same ilk. This is an image of privatism and independence rather than of community and interdependence. The solution to the problems he raises is neither to abandon the artisan metaphor nor to abandon the concept of teaching as craft for a bureaucratic or technical one. Instead, the image of artisanship needs to be redefined given what we now know constitutes good teaching. Independent artisan teachers, for example, can be viewed as a group of *interdependent* artisans who share common goals, who are committed to each other morally, and who function as members of a community of practice.

Communities of Practice

In Chapter Four community of practice was mentioned as the benchmark for defining how deep community is in a school. Developing a community of practice may be the single most important way to improve a school. It is, for example, an effective way to build intellectual capital and intellectual capital, in turn, is directly related to the development of human capital.

Jacob Bronowski (1978) points out, for example, that during Leonardo da Vinci's lifetime (1452–1519) no scientific society existed. Neither Galileo nor Decartes had been born. "And one reason why prolific, imaginative, and inventive brains like Leonardo's failed to make an impact on the body of science was there were no colleagues. . . . Even that tremendous mind could not work in isolation" (p. 123). Bronowski says further that "what has made science successful as a social leaven over the last three hundred years is its change from the practice of individuals, however great their ingenuity, to a communal enterprise" (p. 123). By contrast, Leonardo had colleagues in painting—he was part of a community of practice and his work was undoubtedly better as a result! We can expect the same results from teachers in the schools as communities of practice develop.

Within communities of practice, individual practices of teachers are not abandoned but are connected to each other in such a way that a single shared practice of teaching emerges. High levels of trust, openness, and sharing that revolve around a common focus and a common commitment to teaching and learning characterize this practice. Teachers learn together, share together, and research their practice together. They feel obliged to help each other learn and thus to share their own learning by connecting it to the learning of other members of the community. A community of practice, thus, can be defined as "a group of professionals, informally bound to one another through exposure to a common class of problems, common pursuit of solutions, and thereby themselves embodying a store of knowledge" (Brook Manville cited in Stewart, 1997, p. 96).

Capacity Building

The theme of this chapter has been a simple one. Teachers count in helping schools be effective. But whether they will help students in a particular school or not depends on whether they are invested with enough discretion to act, get the support they need to teach, are involved in continuous learning, and are led by effective leaders. These factors are particularly important in transforming dysfunctional into functional schools. As Ron Wolk explains, "The only sure way to transform dysfunctional schools into effective schools is to build capacity in them—to provide smart, strong leadership, a mission clearly and intensely focused on children's learning, highly competent and committed teachers, clear lines of responsibility, adequate financial resources, and an environment that fosters collaboration, trust, and continuous learning" (Pew Forum on Educational Reform, 1998, p. 46). Building capacity among teachers and focusing that capacity on students and their learning is the critical factor. Continuous capacity building and continuous focusing is best done within communities of practice.

Capacity Building in Practice

What does capacity building and focus look like in practice? Maya Suryaraman's account of events in San Jose's Evergreen Elementary School District provides one vivid example. Her account, published in the *San Jose Mercury News*, shows how a school district can use local resources to support, energize, and grow the character and life-worlds of its schools.

As Suryaraman explains, California state officials consider the Evergreen Elementary School District to be so successful that in 1997 fourteen of its fifteen campuses were designated as California Distinguished Schools. Six of the district schools were nominated by the state to receive the 1997 National Blue Ribbon Award sponsored by the U.S. Department of Education, and five of the six nominated schools eventually received the coveted award. (Nationally, only 262 public and private elementary schools were recognized in 1997.)

The Evergreen district believes that giving teachers the power they need to make decisions is fundamental. But it takes more than power. It takes empowerment—a deliberate effort on the part of the district to provide the direction, support, resources, training, and other means to enable teachers to use their discretion successfully for kids. Suryaraman's account of this highly successful school district is presented as Exhibit 7.2.

Exhibit 7.2. School District Achieves Lots with Little.

When Dove Hill School needed space for a new first-grade classroom this fall, teachers at the campus met and decided to offer up their faculty room. Now they eat their lunch in the back of the library.

"We tried to think what would be best for students," said Alma Hughes, who teaches first grade at the school in San Jose's Evergreen Elementary School District.

In Evergreen—where schools consistently rack up academic awards and students outperform their peers across the county, state and nation—putting kids first and giving teachers power to make decisions are fundamental. They're keys to the district's success.

Exhibit 7.2. School District Achieves Lots with Little, cont'd.

State officials consider Evergreen schools so exemplary that they have named 14 of the district's 15 campuses California Distinguished Schools. Now the state is nominating six of the district's schools—more than in any other California elementary district—for the 1997 National Blue Ribbon awards recognizing outstanding schools.

Across the nation, parents fear that public schools are not educating their children for today's economy.

School improvement efforts often get mired in controversy. Debate rages over "whole language" vs. phonics, bilingual education vs. English-only instruction, and even over how high schools should schedule classes.

Yet Evergreen appears to have found the secret to incorporating new ideas while retaining traditional approaches. Arguably, it is producing results—though it has little money to spend and lots of poor and immigrant children to educate.

"They have lots of what are euphemistically called challenges," said Carol Kennedy, who coordinates the state Department of Education's Distinguished Schools awards program. "Yet here they are, chugging along like 'the little engine that could'—and making it."

Because school funding is based on a complicated formula, Evergreen receives less than $3,900 for each child it educates. That places it second from the bottom of funding in Santa Clara County, even though nearly a fifth of its students come from families on welfare and may need extra help to succeed.

A quarter are immigrants. They come to the district from a long list of countries, including Vietnam, Mexico, Cambodia, India and the Philippines. They must learn a new language as well as their ABCs. And yet, on the 1994 state achievement tests, Evergreen's children outperformed the state average. More telling, in three of six areas, Evergreen students also posted better results than Santa Clara County, which as a whole is more affluent.

After the state discontinued the California Learning Assessment System test amid political controversy in late 1994, Evergreen began giving its students a nationally used standardized test. In all areas, its students are scoring at or above the national norm.

What gives?

For one thing, Evergreen does have some cards in its favor. It is a growing district with continually increasing funding, which has built three new schools in the past decade. It gets a constant influx of new teachers who bring fresh ideas. And it pays them well. Teacher salaries, averaging $46,000 a year, are the second-highest among the county's elementary districts. Stability helps a lot.

Stable leadership buffers teachers from constant shifts in direction. The superintendent, Jim Smith, began in the district as a young teacher in 1962

Exhibit 7.2. School District Achieves Lots with Little, cont'd.

and became superintendent in 1975. Every school board member has served for at least nine years; one trustee was elected as far back as 1967.

But enrollment growth and stable leadership are only part of the picture.

Evergreen fits the profile of effective schools developed by the Menlo Park-based think tank SRI, after it sent researchers to 32 campuses across the nation in 1990–91. The SRI researchers found that successful schools share four elements:

- They give teachers a say in decisions that affect the classroom.
- They set high expectations for all students.
- They nurture collaboration among teachers.
- And they provide focused opportunities for professional growth.

Evergreen tries to do all this while maintaining a continuous internal discussion of how well it's doing. The district sets goals and measures whether it has reached them.

Each year, the district and its schools focus on one subject area. Through meetings, staff members pick apart what students should know, how they are performing and ways to improve.

Richard Cirigliano has visited schools across Santa Clara Valley as an instructor in and former director of San Jose State University's teacher-placement program. He says accountability is one thing that sets Evergreen apart.

"They say what they're going to do, they do it, and then they have someone checking to make sure it's done," said Cirigliano.

All curriculum is written by committees of teachers. Administrators guide the discussion, share research, and point out effective programs in other schools—but they don't make final textbook decisions.

"If I want Book X and the committee wants Book Y, we go with Book Y," said Maryann Cavallo, assistant superintendent for instruction. "But our children must achieve. That's not negotiable."

Teachers such as Rebeca Robbins say setting high standards—and providing ways to reach them—is a pervasive element of Evergreen's culture.

Robbins, a special-education teacher at Cadwallader School, recalls her former principal, Susan Hanna, who last year became the district's director of curriculum. "In every meeting, in every discussion, her question was always, 'How do you do it excellently?'" Robbins said, "It was so consistent."

To support students and teachers, many Evergreen campuses assign teachers coaches they can consult if they run into roadblocks with particular students. If the teacher and the coach are stymied, the child's case gets kicked up to a

Exhibit 7.2. School District Achieves Lots with Little, cont'd.

team of on-campus specialists who consult with the child's parents and draft a plan of action.

So when Alma Hughes of Dove Hill encountered a first-grade student who didn't know his colors—an important pre-academic skill most students have mastered by that point—she brought in her coach and the schoolwide team. Based on the results of testing, the student was given special-education services to help him catch up.

"You could wonder, has this child been living in a closet?" said Hughes. "But the fact is, the child doesn't know his colors, and we have to take him from there."

Throughout the district, Wednesdays before or after school are slotted for teachers to brainstorm strategies and for schools to hold staff meetings. Everyone's always learning.

Elementary teachers also get Thursday afternoons for more collaboration, and to attend workshops coordinated by the district and individual schools. Students put in longer hours four days a week so that school can let out early on Thursdays.

Evergreen also gears its training to its current focus. This year it's math. At a recent Thursday session, fifth-grade teachers picked up ideas and materials for strengthening students' skills in three-dimensional geometry.

Other districts also set aside time for teacher training. But Evergreen's staff development is a coordinated, focused and regular effort.

"The whole district has outstanding training for its teachers," said Barbara Wilson, a consultant with the state Department of Education. She visited Holly Oak School in 1995 to see whether it was worthy of being named a California Distinguished School. It made the cut.

8

Deep Change and the Power of Localism

We have been through several waves of school reform since the publication of *A Nation at Risk* (National Commission on Excellence in Education) in 1983. The waves have brought many new structures, programs, and systems to our schools. As a result, schools look a little different and people within them speak a different language, but deep change is slow in coming (see Newmann, Marks, and Gamoran, 1995; Marks and Louis, 1997; and Elmore, Peterson, and McCartney, 1996). Deep change involves changes in fundamental relationships, in understandings of subject matter, pedagogy, and how students learn, in teachers' skills and behavior, and in student performance.

Defying Physical Laws

There are many reasons why schools are slow to change in deep ways. Quartz (1995) believes, for example, that existing patterns of teaching and learning endure because schools are characterized by a "dominant culture of stabilizing reform" that refines existing teaching practices but does not allow for radical changes to occur (p. 240). This explains why, despite the introduction of so many changes, schooling has remained stable over time. Defying physical laws, schools have managed to change while remaining stable.

How is it possible for stability and change to co-exist? Many experts believe that schools absorb changes without altering underlying forms and assumptions. This reflects Karl Mannheim's (1940) observation that human beings and their institutions have a tendency to understand new things in terms of existing categories. It also reflects James March and Herbert Simon's (1958) "principle of uncertainty absorption," which explains the tendency of schools to understand new things in the same old ways. The story is often told, for example, about the high school teacher who endorsed the change to ninety-minute class periods by explaining that now he would be able to show the whole proverbial film in one class. Throughout rural America one finds examples of small high schools that operate exactly like large high schools. And all of us know of junior high schools that become middle schools but continue to function like junior high schools.

The large high school, a common fixture across the landscape of the urban and suburban United States, provides still another example of how the culture of stabilizing reform works. Despite overwhelming evidence that large high schools do not work well for most students, we continue to build them. Klonsky (1996) summarizes some of the findings from research that supports small high schools as follows:

- Small schools encourage teachers to innovate and "take ownership" of the curriculum.

- Small school size improves students' grades and test scores.

- Small school size greatly improves attendance rates and lowers dropout rates.

- Female and nonwhite students, in particular, do better in smaller schools.

- Students with special needs, including so-called "at-risk," "exceptional," "disadvantaged," and "gifted" students, are better served by smaller school units.

- In the small school environment, security improves and violence decreases, as do student alcohol and drug abuse [p. 2].

Findings similar in importance to these would revolutionize the practice of medicine, architecture, and other fields. The typical response of schools, however, has been not to change by organizing large schools into smaller units or by committing to building new smaller schools. Instead they beef up security, add advisory periods, assign more counselors to the freshman class, buy metal detectors, in-service the teachers, and struggle to make the large high school work better. The emphasis is on tinkering at the edges in such a way that the old form and the existing categories that define the large high school are preserved.

Reculturing Schools

Schools remain stable because the existing culture contains norms that define, and then provide, meaning for parents, teachers, and other locals. These collective meanings help teachers make sense of their existing practices, affirm their sense of purpose, and help them to rationally accept the social situations they experience in schools. For this reason, experts such as Michael Fullan (1991) point out that changes in relationships, teaching practice, and student learning involve changes in school culture.

Reculturing schools, however, is both complex and difficult. Before school cultures can change, individually and collectively held meanings experienced by teachers and students must change. This is true for parents and other locals in the school community as well. Perhaps things would be different if it were possible to move instantly from one set of meanings to another. It is the period in between that often causes the difficulty. Changing a culture requires that people, both individually and collectively, move from something familiar and important into an empty space. And then, once they are in this empty space, they are obliged to build a new set of meanings and norms and a new cultural order to fill up the space. Deep change, in other words, requires the reconstructing of existing individual and collective mindscapes of practice.

How Mindscapes Work

Mindscapes are implicit mental frames through which the reality of schooling and our place in it are envisioned. The assessment and evaluation themes discussed in Chapters Five and Six provide examples of how mindscapes work in shaping policy and in deciding what schools should do and how they should do it. Different approaches to assessment and evaluation, for example, are in part a function of different mindscapes. Approaches to assessment and evaluation can be grouped into three broad categories—standards-referenced, criterion-referenced, and personally referenced (see Eisner, 1991, pp. 101–113; Sergiovanni and Starratt, 1998, pp. 224–226):

1. *Standards-referenced assessment and evaluation* seeks to establish the extent to which teachers and schools measure up to some pre-existing and common standards or definitions of effectiveness. These externally imposed standards are presumed to represent minimum levels of competency that provide a yardstick for comparing teachers and schools to other teachers and schools measured by the same standards.

When applied to teacher evaluations, for example, an instrument is typically used that records the presence or absence of teaching behaviors and other characteristics to track whether teachers are following protocols thought to define effective teaching. Since reliability is very important in standards-referenced evaluation, each evaluation should be able to be duplicated by another evaluator. To achieve this kind of reliability it is important to rule out the judgments of evaluators. Though called an evaluation, standards-referenced teaching evaluation is really a measurement task that is "evaluator proof."

2. *Criterion-referenced assessment and evaluation* seeks to establish the extent to which a school's practice and the practice of its teachers embodies certain standards, goals, purposes, and values set by and considered important to the school. Assuming that the following questions reflect a particular school's shared purposes and values, such an assessment might ask: Does the teacher provide a classroom climate that encourages openness and inquiry? Do teachers accept students without question as individuals? Do teachers teach for understanding? Are students functioning as "workers" and are teachers functioning as "facilitators" or managers of the teaching and learning environment? Do students have responsibility for setting learning goals and deciding on learning strategies? Is cooperation emphasized over competition? Is diversity respected? Are there measurable and other indicators of student learning that match the school's own standards, goals, and objectives? Different school purposes and values would lead to different assessment questions.

When applied to teacher evaluations, the evaluation takes the form of an inquiry that is constructed around issues deemed important by teachers and their supervisors. Questions that guide this inquiry might include: Does the teacher's practice reflect school values? Are there better ways to do it? What is the worth of a particular school value in the first place? Since criterion-referenced teacher evaluation does not lend itself to lists of teaching behaviors to be checked, other forms of supervision such as inquiry, action research, portfolio development, and peer review are better options.

3. *Personally referenced assessment and evaluation* provides the wiggle room that allows administrators, teachers, and students the opportunity to set personal goals and to make comparisons between

past and present performance given these goals. No external standards or norms are used to provide a baseline for making these comparisons. Instead the purpose is to help principals, teachers, and students to understand and critically appraise their performance in light of their own preferences, purposes, goals, beliefs, and the standards they set for their performance.

In today's climate of reform, criterion-referenced assessment and evaluation and personally referenced assessment and evaluation may be the more powerful means to bring about change and may be more protective of the lifeworlds of teachers, students, and parents. But as policy mindscapes they are subordinate to standards-referenced assessment and evaluation. Despite rhetoric about local control, most states use standards-referenced assessment and evaluation approaches when thinking about and crafting strategies for school reform. This mindscape problem leads to certain basic contradictions between what we say we want to accomplish and the strategies we actually use to accomplish these goals.

Contradictions in Change Goals and Strategies

The following ideas are widely shared among policymakers, educational practitioners, parents, and voters: Change that counts is change that affects teaching and learning, helps students developmentally, helps teachers be more effective, and improves the civic life of students in schools. What is not shared are ideas about the ways we should work to bring about the changes that will help schools be more effective.

Imagine having a chance to visit with your state senator and representative, the mayor of your town, your governor, the superintendent of schools, someone from your state education department, some principals and teachers, and a half dozen ordinary citizens about the best ways to improve schools. You ask each person at your meeting to share their ideas about how to bring about changes in the schools. It is very likely that you will be able to sort their ideas into one or more of the following strategy categories:

- Mandate that schools do certain things thought to result in improvements or that schools meet standardized outcomes. Then provide a management system complete with supervision, evaluation, and penalties for noncompliance to back up the mandates for change.

- Rely on corporate images of vision and leadership to motivate, inspire, or otherwise persuade schools to change.

- Apply market theories and principles to schools. Then allow the "invisible hand" of competition, backed up by rewards for winners, to do its work in bringing about change.

- Invest in capacity building that increases teacher professionalism. Then allow professionalism to increase the willingness and ability of teachers to change.

- Work to change the culture of schools by helping them to become covenantal and democratic communities that compel teachers and schools to change.

The answers a person chooses depend in part on how that person understands the nature of schools and human nature itself. Different understandings among policymakers, school officials, and others lead to different policies, strategies, and practices. But not all of these policies, strategies, and practices are equally effective. Deep change results from approaches that match the unique cultural requirements of schools, including their lifeworlds, and that match the unique operational requirements for new teaching and learning, including their systemsworlds.[3]

Formal and Social Organizations

Schools, for example, are typically understood as formal organizations that share characteristics and features with other formal organizations. This generic view of schools allows for easy transfer to the school of assumptions and practices that are found to work elsewhere. Thus, strategies for change that work well in the corporate world and in other sectors of our society are generally assumed to apply to the school (Sergiovanni, 1996). This is why corporate restructuring images of downsizing, standards setting, accountability, and increased competition play such a large role in school reform efforts and why images from other sectors of our society (the worlds of civic and social enterprises, such as families, faith communities, volunteer groups, and mutual aid societies) are often overlooked.

Many experts in organizational theory, however, do not agree with the view that all organizations are the same. Instead they take the view that formal organizations represent only one of several ways in which humans organize themselves and relate to each other. Blau and Scott (1962), for example, make an important distinction between social organizations and formal organizations. They point out that "we would not call a family an organization [meaning formal organization], nor would we so designate a friendship clique, or a community, or an economic market, or the political institutions of our society" (p. 2). To them what differentiates formal organizations from more social enterprises is how human conduct is socially organized. In social organizations, according to Blau and Scott, the structure of social relations and the shared beliefs and orientations that unite members and guide their conduct are important, for they make the whole greater than the sum of its parts. Blau and Scott refer to these dimensions as networks of social relations or shared orientations. The dimensions are similar to community concepts such as social structure and culture. The DNA of social organizations is their lifeworlds. Social organizations thrive when their lifeworlds drive the systemsworld and suffer when the systemsworld colonizes the lifeworld.

Bureaucracies, Markets, and Clans

As a further example, Ouchi (1980) identifies three different kinds of organizations: bureaucracies, markets, and clans. Bureaucracies get things done by developing rational systems of expectations, by placing value on member contributions directed to achieving expectations, by providing supervision, rules, and other means to guide and enable the process, and by compensating fairly. Markets get things done by relying on the "natural" interdependence that emerges from interactions among people, characterized by trading compliance for desired incentives. Clans get things done by connecting people to shared values and beliefs, by relying on emergent norms that discourage opportunistic behavior, and by promoting commitment to the common good. In education we can refer to Ouchi's definition of clans as community.

If Blau and Scott, Ouchi, and other experts in organizational theory are right and different types of organizations exist, then a more effective approach in changing schools may be to first identify the organizational type that best fits the school. We could then adopt an approach to understanding change that leads to the development of special change strategies for the school—change strategies that match the school's special leadership and cultural requirements. To put it another way, since educational practices are confirmed and validated by their underlying theories, what seems like reasonable and correct practice may wind up being neither reasonable nor correct if the underlying theory itself is wrong.

But things are not that simple. As our experiment with that diverse group of people we gathered and quizzed about school change suggests, we do not agree. Different people view schools differently. Schools as bureaucracies, markets, and communities all have their champions. These different ways of understanding schools reflect beliefs that create different change realities. These realities become the basis for how we think and for the change policies and practices we create and use to reform schools. Different views, for example, rely on different change forces for leveraging change. "Force" implies strength or energy brought to bear to leverage or move something or to resist movement. Force can be a form of power understood in physical terms, organizational conventions understood in bureaucratic terms, mental strength or attraction understood in psychological terms, felt obligations understood in moral terms, and so on. Fullan (1993) coined the term *change forces* to communicate similar meanings.

Change Forces

Six change forces can be identified: bureaucratic, personal, market, professional, cultural, and democratic. Each of these forces is related to the different strategies discussed earlier and each prescribes different practices to implement change:

- Examples of bureaucratic forces are rules, mandates, and other requirements intended to provide direct supervision, standardized work processes, or standardized outcomes that are used to prescribe change.

- Examples of personal forces are the personalities, leadership styles, and interpersonal skills of change agents that are used to motivate change.

- Examples of market forces are competition, incentives, and individual choice theories that are used to motivate change.

- Examples of professional forces are standards of expertise, codes of conduct, collegiality, felt obligations, and other professional norms intended to build professional community that is used to compel change.

- Examples of cultural forces are shared values, goals, and ideas about pedagogy, relationships, and politics intended to build covenantal community that is used to compel change.

- Examples of democratic forces are democratic social contacts and shared commitments to the common good intended to build democratic community that is used to compel change.

Those who identify with the school as a formal organization favor bureaucratic and personal forces. Those who view schools as a particular kind of social organization—a learning community— favor professional, cultural, and democratic forces. Market forces, by contrast, are not organizationally oriented at all. Instead they are advocated by policymakers and citizens who believe that schools are complex organizational structures that require bureaucratic rules and that direct leadership should be replaced by the "invisible hand" of competition in the form of incentives and individual choice.

The deciding factor in determining whether change strategies are likely to be successful is their ability to influence key mediating variables in the change equation. These variables include the extent to which teachers are connected to shared norms that support proposed changes; the extent to which teachers understand differently the subjects they teach; the extent to which teachers have an expanded understanding of how students learn; and the extent to which teachers have the necessary skills to teach differently. If these key mediating variables are not influenced positively, then whatever changes do occur in schools will most likely be structural rather than deep and will not sustain themselves over time.

Bureaucratic, personal, and market forces generally result in changes in school structure. Professional, cultural, and democratic forces, on the other hand, being tightly connected to the mediating variables, are more likely to result in deep changes.

Theories of Human Nature

Just as views of schools as either organizations, markets, or communities influence which change strategies are chosen, so do different views of human nature. Choosing a change force makes a statement about how governors, legislators, and other policymakers view people, their capacities, their moral propensities, and their motivational nature.

Most change agents operate from simple theories of human nature. They tend to believe that people are either largely inclined toward good or toward evil. The first inclination represents the "unconstrained view" of human nature and the second inclination represents the "constrained view" (Sowell, 1987).

Change agents who hold the unconstrained view believe that principals, teachers, and other locals can be trusted to act morally and therefore must be provided with the freedom to optimize their propensity to do what is right. Locals have both the capacity and the need to sacrifice their self-interest for valued causes and conceptions of the common good. Teachers, for example, are thought capable of behaving as professionals who willingly accept responsibility for their own practice and who commit themselves to the learning needs of their students.

Within the constrained view, by contrast, it is believed that principals, teachers, and other locals will act selfishly if given the chance. Their primary concern is to maximize their self-interest. Thus constraints in the form of incentives and penalties must be provided to force them to do the right thing. Teachers, for example, may have the capacity to do the right thing, they reason, but this capacity will only be motivated if constraints are provided.

Constrained Change Forces

Bureaucratic and personal change forces both embody the constrained view. Bureaucratic forces seek to motivate by relying on penalties for teachers who will not implement changes. Personal forces seek to motivate by relying on rewards for teachers who will implement changes. In each case the idea is to trade something that teachers and schools want, or want to avoid, for their compliance with proposed changes.

Market forces, too, rely on trades. But these trades do not require a great deal of administration by formal organizational arrangements. Nor do they require much leadership intervention. Instead rational choice theory is used. This theory, detailed later in the chapter, relies on the propensity of people to function as individuals who seek to "maximize their gains and cut their losses" in an open marketplace. Rational choice theory believes it is self-interest that motivates teachers and schools to change.

Since principals and teachers play in this market as individuals, how can systemic change be implemented by using market forces? Wouldn't self-interest work against the common good and provide instead a pattern of willy-nilly changes? Market advocates respond to questions of this kind by noting that the common good defies defining by bureaucratic means or by visionary leadership (or for that matter by shared covenants as assumed by community advocates). Instead the common good is defined by an aggregation of individual preferences. When the market game is played some individuals win and other individuals lose. But on the whole, and over time, it is believed that benefits accrue for everyone and it is these benefits that define the common good.

Rational Choice Theory

Rational choice theory dominates the way most people view human nature. The origins of rational choice theory are found in the fields of economics, evolutionary biology, and behavioral psychology. From economics comes the image of "economic man" who is always in pursuit of self-interest and is never satisfied with what has been accumulated. Economic men and women operate alone, meaning that the drive to maximize gains and cut losses is pursued without regard for the welfare of others.

Adam Smith's *Wealth of Nations* (1937) is considered to be the seminal text for rational choice theory. Smith's speculations emphasized that the individual pursuit of self-interest could be and needed to be harvested to serve moral interests and purposes. The means to this harvest, he proposed, is a system of incentives and penalties designed to constrain humankind's selfish nature.

Charles Darwin's (1985) theories of natural selection expanded the emphasis on competition that plays a major role in market change force strategies. Competition, he argues, weeds out the weak players, thus making the pool of survivors and new replacements for the weak stronger over time. Self-interest motivates competitive play. Darwin's theory provides the script for many school choice proposals that are based solely on free market principles.

Behavioral psychology contributed the "law of effect" (Skinner, 1953) to the market change forces equation. According to the law of effect, human behavior is controlled by past consequences. Thus having received a reward or punishment in the past we are conditioned to repeat the behavior again and again to get the reward and to avoid the punishment.

One particular variation of rational choice theory is "agency theory" (Moe, 1984). Agency theory assumes that the interests of managers and workers are not the same. Workers are interested in the best deal for the least effort. Managers are interested in the best performance at the least cost. Managers are dependent upon workers who have more information about how to do the job. Given the choice, workers will take advantage of this situation. Thus managers must use checks and balances and rewards and punishments to control and motivate workers (Bimber, 1993). Agency theory fits school change by substituting change agent for manager and teacher for worker, or the state for manager and the local school site for worker. Not only are teachers not trusted by their supervisors but local school communities are not trusted by their state governments.

Unconstrained Change Forces

Professional, cultural, and democratic change forces embody the unconstrained view of human nature. Professional forces, for example, rely on professional training, standards of practice, and norms for behavior that, once internalized, are thought to compel change. Change behavior is motivated by professional virtues that function as substitutes for bureaucratic, personal, and market change forces (Sergiovanni, 1994). One professional virtue is a commitment by principals and teachers to practice in an exemplary way by staying abreast of new developments, researching their own practice, trying out new approaches, and otherwise accepting responsibility for their own development. Another professional virtue is to accept responsibility not only for one's own individual practice but for the practice of teaching that exists in the school. Embodiment of this virtue transforms teaching from a collection of individual teaching practices to a single and shared practice of teaching. As teachers come to share the same practice, a third virtue, colleagueship, comes into play. Colleagueship is not merely congenial relationships or patterns of working together but is connection through morally held webs of obligations and commitments. Taken together the professional virtues enable the development of professional community.

Change agents who rely on cultural change forces believe that schools can become communities in their own right. Schools can become covenantal learning communities with cultures that compel changes among teachers and students that result in better teaching and learning. Cultural change forces rely on community norms, values, and ideas that, when internalized, speak to everyone in a moral voice. Teachers, students, and other members of this community, they argue, are motivated by felt obligations that emerge from the shared values and norms that define the school as a covenantal community (see Etzioni, 1988; Sergiovanni, 1994).

Democratic change forces rely on commitment to democratic social contracts that function to guide school decision making and to provide for patterns of obligations and duties that compel change. This strategy seeks to transform teachers and students into "citizens" committed to civic virtue. Civic virtue, defined as the willingness to sacrifice one's self-interest for the common good, is a key pillar undergirding American, Canadian, and other democracies with similar political and moral traditions.

Professional, cultural, and democratic change forces all share the purpose of building community in schools as a means of implementing deep changes. When used together the three change forces seek to transform schools from organizations or markets to professional, learning, and democratic communities.

As suggested in Chapter Four, schools become communities when they are able to cultivate community of mind that becomes the source of authority for making decisions, establishing norms, and otherwise directing human behavior (Sergiovanni, 1994). Professional, cultural, and democratic change forces help create a community of mind by emphasizing ideas that define professional relationships and responsibilities, that define broader questions of purpose, relationships, and behavior, and that define the democratic ideal as the standard for making decisions. All three contribute to the school's moral voice that calls upon teachers, parents, and students alike to respond on behalf of the common good.

Consequences

Which change forces work for the school? That depends on how the question is framed. If the question is framed as "What works in bringing about changes in school structures and arrangements?" then the answer is change forces that are based on views of schools as either formal organizations or as markets. But when the question is framed as "What works in schools over the long term?" or "What works for implementing deep changes in schools?" then the answer is change forces that are based on views of schools as communities. At root, deep changes involve changing school cultures. And changing school cultures requires changes in meanings that are individually and collectively held by teachers—requirements more likely to be met in schools understood as communities. Change strategies, their characteristics, and consequences are summarized in Table 8.1.

Why Community Theories Instead of Market Theories?

Most reformers seem to agree that change forces based on conceptions of the school as a formal bureaucratic organization are not very effective. Some reformers are also unhappy with the use of personal change forces that emerge from conceptions of the school as a formal organic organization. The way to break out of this organizational thinking, they believe, is to look more and more to market forces that view schools and teachers as commodities within a free marketplace (Chubb and Moe, 1990).

Many advocates of market change forces seem comfortable with community ideas. They argue that while the promotion of community-oriented schools cannot be guaranteed as the outcome of using rational choice theory in a free market setting, it is a possible and perhaps even likely outcome. Teachers, students, and their parents, they argue, would have free choice in an open market to build community-oriented schools. All they need is to be successful enough to win as they compete with other conceptions of schooling. Such reasoning has appeal. But, as discussed below, the prospects for the success of market forces over the long run are dim unless choice is viewed differently than is now the case. Now choice is viewed as an economic concept oriented to the maximizing of one's self-interest. If choice were viewed instead as a civic concept oriented to defining and then serving the common good, there might be a way of incorporating market ideas into the community view.

Market forces, for example, may be more efficient than democratic forces, but they may not be appropriate given schools' special importance and their responsibility to promote societal interests.

Table 8.1. Change Forces, Characteristics, and Consequences.

Change Forces	Change Practices	Theories of Human Nature	Change Consequences
Bureaucratic	1. Rely on rules, mandates, and requirements to provide direct supervision, standardized work processes, and/or standardized outcomes to prescribe change.	*Constrained:* The visible hand of rational choice theory linked to penalties is necessary to motivate change.	School changes just enough to avoid sanctions. Change stops when sanctions are removed.
Personal	2. Rely on personality, leadership style, and interpersonal skills of change agents to motivate change.	*Constrained:* The visible hand of rational choice theory linked to psychological rewards is necessary to motivate change.	School changes just enough to receive gratification of needs. Change stops when rewards are not available.
Market	3. Rely on competition, incentives, and individual choice to motivate change.	*Constrained:* The invisible hand of rational choice theory linked to individual self-interest is necessary to motivate change.	School changes just enough to win in the marketplace. Winning becomes less important after repeated losses.
Professional	4. Rely on standards of expertise, codes of conduct, collegiality, felt obligations, and other professional norms to build professional community.	*Unconstrained:* The visible hand of professional socialization provides standards of practice and norms that compel change.	School internalizes norms of competence and virtue that compel change.
Cultural	5. Rely on shared values, goals and ideas about pedagogy, relationships, and politics to build covenantal community.	*Unconstrained:* The invisible hand of community norms, values, and ideas speak in a moral voice to compel change.	School internalizes community norms that compel change.
Democratic	6. Rely on democratic social contracts and shared commitments to the common good to build democratic community.	*Unconstrained:* The invisible hand of democratic traditions and internalized norms compel change.	School internalizes democratic norms that compel change.

Source: Adapted from Sergiovanni, 1998, in Hargreaves, Lieberman, Fullan, and Hopkins (eds.), *International Handbook of Educational Change*, Part I, pp. 571–596. Published with kind permission from Kluwer Academic Publishers.

Choice is an important feature in both market and democratic images of schools. In markets, individuals, motivated by self-interest, act alone in making preferred choices. Democratic choice, by contrast, is collective, complex, cumbersome, time-consuming, and sometimes combative. Further, and unlike market choices where the will of the majority is not supposed to be imposed on everyone, once a democratic decision is made it applies to everyone.

Despite inefficiencies, democratic decision making should be preferred for the things that society values—things like defense, legal codes, transportation, and health care. "When, however, the things we are talking about are trivial—designer jeans, compact discs, deodorant soaps, different types of breakfast cereals—then democratic decision making is a waste of effort. . . . [D]emocratic politics should be the system we use for the distribution of everything important, and economic markets should be the system we use for the distribution of everything trivial" (Schwartz, 1994, p. 21). Given this reasoning, schools belong in the first category.

Democratic choice is an essential ingredient in building community within a diverse society. In Chapter Four, for example, the ideas of creating communities within community and neighborhoods within schools are strong metaphors for organizing schools in ways that enable diverse people to come together to serve the common good. This vision of schooling cannot be realized without incorporating choice. If schools are to be redefined as collections of people and ideas, thus making it possible for any school building to house several independent and semi-independent schools side by side, then students and their families, as well as teachers, should be able to choose the particular school or school within school they wish to join.

The Power of Localism

In summary, the strategies for change that might make sense for some sectors of our society may not work well for other sectors. Schools are a case in point. Deep changes in schools are difficult to achieve when using change forces that emerge from views of schools as formal bureaucratic organizations, formal organic organizations, or markets. This difficulty is exacerbated by the negative effects that constrained theories and practices can have on teachers. Instead of nurturing professional community, constrained views breed cynicism, erode civic virtue, and encourage the development of human nature's selfish side at the expense of human nature's altruistic side. Yet the voluminous literature on change in schools gives scant attention to this problem.

Deep changes may well require two things: first, that the basic metaphor for the school itself be changed to that of a community. And once this is done, leadership strategies and change forces must be matched to the unique cultural requirements of schools understood as communities.

Not only is this approach practical and effective for bringing about changes that will improve schools but it is practical and effective politically as well. After all, most Americans want community for their schools. Most Americans trust the teachers who work in their schools and believe in localism. A recent survey of one thousand Californians, for example, revealed that most had confidence in school reform efforts led by parents and teachers (Johnston, 1998). In responding to the question "Whom do you trust most to reform schools and raise children's achievement?" parents and teachers together accounted for 65 percent of the responses, as compared with only 17 percent for the state government. The lifeworlds of schools, it appears, are very much on the minds and in the hearts of most Americans—an observation, I suspect, that resonates in other cultures as well.

9

Leadership, Democracy, and the Lifeworld

"Some're balls and some're strikes and I calls 'em as I sees 'em," said the first umpire. "Some're balls and some're strikes and I calls 'em as they *are*," said the second umpire. "Well," said the third, "some're balls, all right, and sure, some're strikes. But until I call 'em they ain't nothin'" (adopted from Kegan and Lahey, 1984, p. 199). The umpires, as Kegan and Lahey point out, were debating different views of the nature of reality and its relationship to the exercise of authority. How we understand these concepts helps shape our view of leadership.

What makes a good leader? That's a tough question. Context plays a key role in deciding whether certain approaches to leadership will be effective or not. Thus what a leader says and does to be effective in one kind of enterprise may not lead to effectiveness in another kind of enterprise. Susan Moore Johnson puts it this way: "Leadership looks different—and is different—depending on whether it is experienced in a legislature, on a battlefield, at a rally, on a factory floor, or in a school district" (1996, p. 14).

Schools need special leadership because schools are special places. Sure schools share with other enterprises common managerial requirements that ensure basic levels of organizational purpose, competence, reliability, structure, and stability. But schools must respond as well to the unique political realities they face. After all schools belong to parents and children, interact with the needs of local businesses, churches, and other community groups, and have a unique relationship with state governments. These "stakeholders" don't always agree, and it takes a high level of political skill for school leaders to bring about the necessary consensus and commitment to make schools work well for everyone.

Schools need special leadership because they are lifeworld-intensive. Values play a particularly important role. As Harry Broudy (1965) reminds us, "The educator, however, deals with nothing but values—human beings who are clusters and constellations of value potentials. Nothing human is really alien to the educational enterprise and there is, therefore, something incongruous about educational administrators evading fundamental value conflicts. . . . The public will never quite permit the educational administrator the moral latitude that it affords some of its servants. For to statesmen and soldiers men entrust their lives and fortunes, but to the schools they entrust their precarious hold on humanity itself" (p. 52). For these reasons school administration, at root, is an ethical science concerned with good or better processes, good or better means, and good or better ends. This immersion of schooling and of school administration in values, preferences, ideas, aspirations, and hopes accentuates the importance of lifeworld concerns of local schools and their constituents. To be ethically responsive the school leader must be vigilant in protecting the lifeworld from being colonized by the systemsworld.

Schools also need special leadership because school professionals don't react warmly to the kind of hierarchically based command leadership or hero leadership that characterizes so many other kinds of organizations. Nor do these professionals have a high tolerance for bureaucratic rituals. Though school leaders may be in charge, the best of them are aware that often the teachers they supervise know more about what needs to be done and how to do it than they do. This reality creates large ability-authority gaps in schools that must be breached (see Sergiovanni, 1999).

Schools are places where children and young people struggle to achieve the necessary developmental growth, intellectual knowledge, practical skills, habits of mind, and character traits that get them ready for engaging in a lifetime of leading and learning. The presence of children and young adults in a learning and developing environment and the responsibility that schools have to serve these students well are still other characteristics that make schools unique and that require us to view school leadership differently. Ordinary images of how to organize, provide leadership and support, motivate, and ensure accountability just do not seem to fit schools very well.

The unique context for schooling, particularly in a democratic society, raises the question of sources of authority for leadership practice. As important as a school leader's personality and interpersonal skills may be to success, and as handy as bureaucratic reasons may be to use, neither is sufficiently powerful to provide that leader with the sources of authority needed to reach students, parents, teachers, and others in powerful ways. Needed are substitutes for bureaucratic and personal leadership that compel people to respond for internal reasons. Substitutes for leadership are exactly what a moral emphasis in leadership can provide.

The chapters in this book describe a kind of moral leadership that I believe must become the framework for the way we do things in schools. This leadership is moral because it emphasizes bringing diverse people into a common cause by making the school a covenantal community. Covenantal communities have at their center shared ideas, principles, and purposes that provide a powerful source of authority for leadership practice. In covenantal communities the purpose of leadership is to create a shared followership. Leaders in covenantal communities function as head followers.

The language of head followership focuses attention on what is being followed. There can be no leadership if there is *nothing* important to follow. For many, *followership* is a pejorative term that embodies hierarchy and implies subordination. This is only true if followership is linked interpersonally to following another person. But when followership is linked to ideas it takes on intellectual and spiritual qualities. Followers of the gospel, followers of the U.S. Constitution and the Bill of Rights, followers of constructivist theories of learning are hardly subordinates but are instead moved by faith in the integrity of ideas and the strength of their commitment to these ideas.

Leadership, in this sense, is more cognitive than interpersonal, and the source of authority for leadership practice is based on goals, purposes, values, commitments, and other ideas that provide the basis for followership. This idea-based leadership is much more likely to motivate people than is interpersonally based leadership. The evidence for this assertion can be found in your own personal experiences.

Imagine a leader whom you personally admire because of her or his ability to handle people well. But you do not agree with this person's goals. Compare this leader with another you may not even like very much but whose ideas make sense to you. Which of the two leaders would you follow? Which of the two leaders is more likely to motivate you to action? If it is the second person, then it appears that admiration, imitation, style, and affection may be less important to followership than agreement on ideas, values, and goals (Wills, 1994). This scenario illustrates the four pillars of leadership: leaders, followers, ideas, and action. All four are needed for leadership to be effective. Leadership that does not result in action, for example, is like a work only half-completed, no matter how eloquent its ideas or passionate its followers. Action is much more likely to result when leaders and followers are connected to each other by a commitment to common ideas.

Figure 9.1 compares the effects of personal attractiveness with shared commitment on subsequent followership. As suggested in the figure, moral leadership and leadership based on shared ideas are more powerful and enduring than leadership based on personality and interpersonal skills. In the upper left-hand quadrant, for exam-

Figure 9.1. Shared Commitments, Personal Attractiveness, and Followership.

	Personally Based Leadership	Morally Based Leadership	
High	Followership may be high as long as P is high P+ I–	Followership is high P+ I+	Low
	Followership is low P– I–	Followership is high even when P is low P– I+	
Low			High

Personal Attractiveness of the Leader (P)

Shared Commitment to Ideas and Values (I)

Source: Sergiovanni, 1998: "Moral Authority, Community and Diversity: Leadership Challenges for the 21st Century."

ple, followership may be high as long as people respond to the leader's personality and leadership style. In the lower right-hand quadrant, by contrast, followership remains high even when personal attractiveness is low. This is because followership is not linked to the leader's personality or style but to valued ideas.

Stories of Leadership and Life

Relying on ideas as the source of leadership authority and appreciating the importance of developing a shared followership brings a cognitive twist to leadership practice. Howard Gardner (1995), for example, views leadership "as a process that occurs within the minds of individuals who live in a culture—a process that entails the capacities to create stories, to understand and evaluate these stories, and to appreciate the struggle among stories. Ultimately, certain kinds of stories will typically become predominant—in particular, stories that provide an adequate and timely sense of identity for individuals who live within a community or institution" (p. 22).

Stories provide us with a sense of purpose and direction, with anchors that help us with questions of identity, and with ways to make sense of our lives and create meaning. Stories help create, nurture, and expand our lifeworlds.

Of course we experience many different kinds of stories in our lives. Some are stories about national politics or foreign policy. Others are stories that influence us at work. But in this book the question at issue has been, where do the stories that affect our personal lives, the moral development of our children, and the processes of schooling come from? Should they come exclusively from laws? Should they come from bureaucratic mandates? Should they come from powerful elites or from high-status commissions? Or should local citizens play the major role in creating these stories for themselves? The answer, of course, is that stories come from many places. But the major story line that helps us to define our personal lives and shape the moral and educational experiences of our children, I have argued, should originate in the many local communities with which we identify and to which we belong.

Lifeworlds address the normative and spiritual questions that define our most intimate relationships with family and friends and these relationships address the spiritual side of schools. As Parker Palmer (1998) explains:

> As a teacher, I have seen the price we pay for a system of education so fearful of things spiritual that it fails to address the real issues of our lives—dispensing facts at the expense of meaning, information at the expense of wisdom. . . . Spiritual questions are the kind that we, and our students, ask every day of our lives as we yearn to connect with the largeness of life: "Does my life have meaning and purpose?" "Do I have gifts that the world wants and needs?" "Whom and what can I trust?" "How can I rise above my fears?" "How do I deal with suffering, my own and that of my family and friends?" "How does one maintain hope?" "What about death?" [pp. 7–8].

The reason for a local emphasis can be explained as follows. It is from our search for answers to the kinds of questions described that our school goals and objectives must be derived, our school designs constructed, our curriculum developed, and our accountability systems crafted, and not the other way around.

Linda Lambert (Lambert and others, 1995) pushes us further toward a lifeworld view of leadership by defining leadership as involving a reciprocal process that enables members of a school community to construct meaning that leads toward a common purpose (p. 33). To her, reciprocal relationships are the means we use to make sense of our own worlds, to continually define ourselves, and to grow together. She refers to this kind of leadership as constructivist and views it as being less a role to be assumed by some and more a function to be assumed by all. Key is the potential of constructivist leadership to build capacity among people and in schools. Schools that are good at helping members construct meaning and craft common purposes are likely to be highly skilled in building capacity and in developing broad participation among members. This combination, Lambert points out, promotes learning and encourages acceptance of a collective responsibility for the success of the school (Lambert, 1998). Linking leadership directly to the construction of meaning, the facilitation of learning, and the development of collective responsibility links leadership directly to the lifeworld of schools.

Leadership and Democratic Values

When the U.S. Constitution of 1787 was debated, two different political conceptions competed with each other. These conceptions represented different views of policy development and of the distribution of leadership authority. Both of these views are still in existence in the United States and in most other countries. Each conception was based on a different view of human nature, a different view of representation by the people, a different set of democratic values, and a different view of procedural democracy. The first conception was that of the *republicans* and the second was that of the *pluralists* (see Sunstein, 1993; see also Chapter 10, "The Politics of Virtue" in Sergiovanni, 1996). The republican view resembled that of modern-day advocates of schools as communities, and the pluralist view resembled that of modern day professional managers who favor large bureaucratic schools and school systems governed by bodies that range from the governor's office to the various administrative offices of the school.

To republicans the world of politics was both direct and deliberate. Citizens running the affairs of government by engaging directly in dialogue and discussion characterized the democratic process. The ideal model was that of the town meeting in which citizens gathered to engage directly in the decisions of the day and to decide their fates. This was a politics of self-rule by the people governed by a commitment to the principle of civic virtue. This principle was defined as the willingness of citizens to sacrifice their self-interest on behalf of the common good. The principle of civic virtue was designed to protect the body politic from capricious majority rule or from selfish personal interests that would press private preferences on others.

The republican perception of politics embodied a rational and altruistic view of human nature that assumed reasonable people were capable of behaving virtuously by doing what was best for all. They believed, as well, that through virtuous dialogue the common good could be identified, that superior values could be revealed, and that practical reasoning could prevail.

Pluralists, on the other hand, were a more suspicious lot. They believed that left to their own devices ordinary people would not behave rationally, would not be able to identify the common good, and would place their own self-interests above the common good. The purpose of politics, therefore, was to prevent, and if necessary referee, a free-for-all struggle among self-interested groups competing for scarce resources. Direct democracy just doesn't work. Instead a reliance on representative democracy, whereby duly elected or duly appointed elites rule, is needed.

To pluralists, politics is a process of bargaining and compromising that is best rationally done by representative government—a government of individuals with preselected interests who resolve their differences as adversaries within a structured political process. The common good, according to pluralists, is not defined beforehand or by consensus of the polity but is defined instead by an aggregation of individual preferences. The views of the winners in this politics of division determine the common good for the losers, the disinterested, the anonymous, and everyone else.

Both republican and pluralist views make sense but for different spheres of our lives. When concerned with such matters of state as the economy, defense, transportation, foreign affairs, and broad educational policy, the view of the pluralists makes sense. But when concerned with such matters as family, spirituality, core values, personal beliefs, and the education of our young people, the republican view makes sense. These family-oriented, community-oriented and other lifeworld-centered arenas of our lives, according to republicans, should be decided locally by the people.

Layered loyalties and shared accountability is one strategy for bringing republican and pluralist views together. This strategy requires individual schools to make promises to the general public in the form of the kind of climate, organizational structure, curriculum, goals, assessments, and outcomes they hope to pursue. The promises would differ from school to school. But, as is the case with other aspects of our lives, promises must be kept. The state would have the primary responsibility for administering an accountability system that assesses the extent to which each school keeps its promises. The whole school quality review process (described in Chapter Six) is an ideal mechanism for such an assessment, since it has the capacity to assess schools differently, individually, and on their own terms. This "promises made, promises kept" system of accountability would operate under a *broad* common framework that would provide an abbreviated set of standards for competencies in a few basic areas of literacy, civility, and managerial efficiency.

The Principle of Subsidiarity

The lifeworld-centered arena of our lives should be governed by the principle of subsidiarity. Formulated by Pope Pius XI, the principle states government "should by its very nature, provide help [subsidium] to members of the body social, it should never destroy or absorb them'" (cited in Hollenbach, 1995, p. 148). The principle of subsidiarity stresses localism through the establishment of self-governing, small-scale communities.

As Robert J. Starratt (1996) explains, "According to this principle the authority to make discretionary decisions concerning the work is placed as close to the work as possible" (p. 121). Operational decisions about schools, for example, are not made in the governor's office, the legislature, or the superintendent's office but in the classrooms. Subsidiarity, according to Starratt (1996), unites authority with responsibility, and by so doing subsidiarity unites decision making with accountability. Starratt believes that the work of teaching and learning cannot be managed from afar without compromising the meaning and significance that defines the lifeworlds of schools.

Central to the concept of subsidiarity is trust and the willingness to distribute power throughout the educational system of a state or a school district (West-Burnham, 1997). To practice this principle, states need to be willing to trust teachers, principals, parents, students, and other locals.

According to Fukuyama (1995, cited in West-Burnham, 1997):

> If people who have worked together in an enterprise trust one another because they are all operating to a common set of ethical norms. . . . Such a society will be better able to innovate organizationally, since the high degree of trust will permit a wide variety of social relationships to emerge. . . .
>
> By contrast, people who do not trust one another will end up co-operating only under a system of formal rules

and regulations, which have to be negotiated, agreed
to, litigated, and enforced, sometimes by coercive means
[p. 242].

Both republican and pluralist views of democracy make sense but
for different spheres of our lives. Both are needed in education.
Pluralist views seem appropriate to decide the broad policies and
frameworks within which local schools must work. Locals, relying
on republican views of democracy embodied in direct involvement
within a provided framework, are free to decide both the means and
ends of schooling for themselves. Republican and pluralist views of
democracy are brought together in the image of a mosaic or of neighborhoods within a city, as described in Chapter Four. Together they
provide the foundation for a school policy system composed of layered loyalties and shared accountability that brings both state and
local stakeholders together as complements in a spirit of mutuality.

Subsidiarity and mutuality together raise an important question
for our governors, legislators, and other policymakers. If we agree
that democracy is good for our country, why not for our schools? I
speak not of representative democracy that ultimately centralizes
shared decision making at the statehouse but genuine, authentic,
direct democracy that gives voice to parents, teachers, students, and
other citizens of the local level. In an authentic system of local control, voice should not be just over means but ends as well.

Rules of Engagement in Local Decision Making

It would be a mistake to assume that within the republican view,
direct democracy among locals in a diverse society will always
be rational and deliberate. Values and emotions count, too (see
Sergiovanni, 1992). Etzioni (1996) proposes certain rules of engagement for talking about values that can help locals maintain civility
and a commitment to the common good while exploring their differences (pp. 104–106). The rules can summarized as follows:

- Contesting parties should not personally attack each other and should refrain from depicting the other side's values as being negative.

- Contesting parties should respect or at least not affront the deepest moral commitments of each other.

- Contesting parties should commit themselves to using less the language of rights and more the language of wants, needs, interests, and responsibilities.

- Contesting parties should agree to leave some issues out of the debate as a way to narrow and focus the conversation, thus making it manageable, and as a way to draw on an existing shared foundation.

Etzioni also quotes James Hunter (1994) in identifying four additional rules: "First, those who claim the right to dissent should assume the responsibility to debate. . . . Second, those who claim the right to criticize should assume the responsibility to comprehend. . . . Third, those who claim the right to influence should accept the responsibility not to inflame. . . . Fourth, those who claim the right to participate should accept the responsibility to persuade" (cited in Etzioni, 1996, pp. 105–106).

The Midwife-Leader

What is the role of principals and other designated leaders in implementing the rules of engagement as problems are identified, differences are discussed, and common ground is sought at the local level? Socrates would suggest that it is that of the "midwife" who knows how to empower and enable others to act together on behalf of the common good: "I am so far like the midwife that I cannot myself give birth to wisdom; and the common reproach is true, that though I question others, I can myself bring nothing to light because there is no wisdom in me. The reason is this: heaven constrains me to serve as a midwife, but has debarred me from giving birth" (Plato, *Theaetetus* cited in Grob, 1984, p. 278). The midwife-leader empowers and enables by generating valid and useful information, encouraging people to make free and informed choices based on this information, and building internal commitment to these choices (see Argyris, 1964, 1965, 1970).

Generating Valid and Useful Information

Reasonably accurate and nonevaluative information about what is actually going on is valid information. Such information helps us to understand factors underlying problems, feelings associated with problems, and how these factors and feelings relate to each other and to other problems that might be under consideration. Objectives, goals, and purposes we value are examples of valid information. A comparison of "real" and "ideal" information often provides us with another kind of valid information composed of distinctions between where we are and where we would like to be.

Usually valid and useful information consists of facts, hard data, and other cognitive information. But often the most important valid information that needs to be generated, discussed, understood, and used deals with feelings, assumptions, fears, values, defenses, and worries that each of us has. Valid information requires a commitment from leaders to be open and frank about their opinions and feelings in a way that helps others to be open and frank. This is quite different than being "honest"—that is, saying exactly what we think regardless of the situation and regardless of how other people feel. Designated leaders will probably need to take the initiative in generating valid information, and as they are successful in this endeavor, responsibility for valid information will become more widespread. Valid information can be judged by the extent to which people are gaining feedback that they find useful; are expressing their own feelings and permitting others to express ideas, feelings, and values; are showing openness to new ideas and taking risks with these ideas.

Free and Informed Choice

Free and informed choice is not the same as the right to choose or not to choose without the benefit of valid information. Instead it results from examining a problem by understanding its cognitive and affective dimensions and then freely choosing a course of action or nonaction. As Argyris (1970) suggests, "A choice is free to the extent the members can make their selections for a course of action with minimal internal defensiveness; can define the path (or paths) by which the intended consequence is to be achieved; can relate the choice to their central needs; and can build into their choices a realistic and challenging level of aspiration. Free choice therefore implies that the members are able to explore as many alternatives as they can consider significant and select those that are central to their needs" (p. 19).

Free and informed choice does not come easy for people who have had little experience with it. Leaders may need to help parents, teachers, students, and other locals to feel comfortable with and competent in exercising free and informed choice. Further, free and informed choice cannot be practiced all the time for all decisions. Often teachers, for example, may not have the appropriate background to meet the informed choice requirement or may not be interested in becoming informed enough to make a free and informed choice. Not everyone, in other words, needs to be involved in everything. But it is important for people to be involved and have the opportunity to make free and informed choices about the things that are important to them.

Building Internal Commitment to Change

Internal commitment builds from free and informed choice and may be the single most important contributor to school effectiveness. Argyris (1970) explains, "Internal commitment means the course of action or choice that has been internalized by each member so that he experiences a high degree of ownership and has a feeling of responsibility about the choice and its implications. Internal commitment means that the individual has reached the point where he is acting on the choice because it fulfills his own needs and sense of responsibility, as well as those of the system" (p. 20).

The idea of leader as midwife is to both empower and enable others to be able to make better decisions about what needs to be done to make the school a better place for teaching and learning. Engaging in enabling others to engage in problem solving and decision making becomes a central concern of the midwife-leader, as illustrated in Figure 9.2.

Note that there are certain ethical principles that the leader needs to follow as he or she engages in the provision of valid information, free and informed choice, and internal commitment. These principles are collaboration, education, experimentation, and task orientation (Benne, 1949). If the leader ignores these principles,

Figure 9.2. The Leader as Midwife.

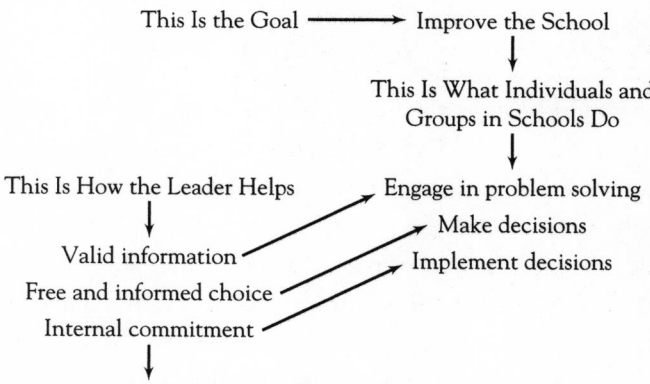

This Is the Goal ⟶ Improve the School

This Is What Individuals and
Groups in Schools Do

This Is How the Leader Helps → Engage in problem solving

→ Make decisions

Valid information → Implement decisions

Free and informed choice

Internal commitment

These Are the Ethical Principles That the Leader Follows
    a. Uses a collaborative process

    b. Gives attention to educational-process goals

    c. Considers change experimental

    d. Has a task-oriented perspective

Source: Sergiovanni and Elliott, 1975, p. 131.

she or he may be engaged in manipulation rather than in empowering and enabling leadership. The first of these principles, collaboration, requires that both designated leaders and followers form a partnership, with each being aware of the intentions of others. Teachers, for example, have a right to know what a principal is up to and why certain goals and actions are being proposed. So do parents and students. Giving attention to the educational process requires that the leader work to free others from depending upon him or her. It is the problem, the issues that are to be dealt with, the substantive work of the school that is the focus of interactions and decisions, the fuel that drives the conversation, the source of authority for what is done. The leader also needs to encourage everyone to consider the changes that are decided upon to be experimental and thus amenable to adjustment if necessary. Finally, the leader needs to be task-oriented in the sense that her or his motivation is not grounded in seeking gains in status, prestige, power, and so on but in a commitment to improving the quality of life that the school provides for everyone.

A Restatement of the Book's Theme

It would be a mistake to assume that the systemsworld is secondary to the lifeworld. Both are important. But both must be in balance for schools to work well. Balance is achieved when the lifeworld of the school determines the systemsworld, and colonization of the lifeworld occurs when the systemsworld determines the lifeworld. The systemsworld provides the instrumental means, the management know-how, the operational systems, and the technical support that help us to achieve our goals, values, and dreams. Without a properly aligned systemsworld our dreams would never become realities. Kao (1996) uses the metaphor of sheet music to describe the systemsworld and how it should work: "A well-managed enterprise can't survive without some sheet music. It allows the management of complexity, without which the modern symphony orchestra . . . would degenerate into cacophony. Most large-scale human interactions require their specific blue-prints, rituals, road maps, scripts, whatever, but they also require improvisation" (cited in West-Burnham, 1997, p. 238).

Bard College President Leon Botstein (1997) equates the life-world with the human quest for hope. In his words:

> [E]ducation is a precondition of hope. Without the com-mand of language, and by inference, thought, ideas, and knowledge—hope disappears or becomes meaningless. Yet when everything else fails we are subjected con-stantly by politicians, religious leaders, and pundits of all types to an appeal to mere "hope."
>
> The consequence of this insight into the nature and meaning of hope is to place education even more into the center as a priority for this country. At stake are not only economic development, social cohesion and stabil-ity, and the health of our national consciousness and political system. Our sense of individual self-worth and the sacred character of life hang in the balance. Hope for ourselves, our children, and our world is contingent on education. Survival depends on education as does free-dom. The time has come to set pessimism aside and cre-ate an educational system in this country adequate to enable future Americans to hope, and with that hope, to take responsibility for themselves and the well being of our society and culture [p. 39].

The lifeworld is the essence of hope. Hope is necessary for our schools to flourish. From education comes hope. Without education there is no hope. Without hope lifeworlds erode. Schools and local communities can be the front line in the defense of hope by main-taining proper balance between the lifeworld and the systemsworld without denying either. As a society we need only to ensure that the former generates the latter. Achieving this balance at all levels of government from the statehouse to the schoolhouse may be the most important purpose of leadership. But achieving this balance will require some new thinking about layered loyalties, layered accountability, and layered allocations of democratic responsibility. Are we up to this new thinking? I think we are.

"Write down the vision clearly upon the tablets so that one can read it widely. For the vision still has its time, presses on to fulfill-ment, and will not disappoint; if it delays, wait for it, it surely will come, it will not be late" (Habakkuk 2:2–4).

Appendix A

Excerpt from an External Review

Following is an excerpt from an external review report for a small K–8 public school that follows the Illinois model. The report is fictional; it follows closely the material that was presented in the exit conference with the internal review team and faculty at the conclusion of the external review. The information was collected by individuals but represents the perspective of the external review team. Illinois Quality Assurance and Planning process focuses on learning. Therefore, we avoid making value judgments or presenting lists of strengths and weaknesses. Instead we provide information that the school can use in further improvement planning.

It is not the intention of this report to evaluate individual members of the school. The entire focus is on *learning*. We offer a summary of our observations and the reflections of the team, highlighting teaching and learning; student learning, progress and achievement; and the school as learning community [this excerpt will focus only on teaching and learning]. We believe that the school is best suited to evaluate its own planning, and the information provided in the following pages should be of considerable value to the school as it engages in this process.

During the visit, members of the team visited classes, conducted interviews, held focus groups, and attended events and meetings. The team also reviewed examples of student work, paying particular attention to the work students did during their lessons, work displayed in classrooms and common areas, and exhibits provided to the external review team. This work represented all grades, all ability levels, and all subject areas found in the curriculum. These exhibits included local assessment results, results of standardized tests, school publications, anecdotal records, and other related materials.

Part 1: Teaching and Learning

The primary mission of schools revolves around themes of teaching and learning. This emphasis, therefore, underpins all other elements of the review process. In the category of teaching and learning the following elements will be considered: (1) the teaching and learning environment, (2) learning processes, (3) teaching and instructional strategies, and (4) student responses.

The mission statement of Lexington Learning Academy states, "Our mission is to offer an exceptional academic program embedded in the communication arts as an integral part of an enriching curriculum that develops students' abilities to communicate effectively, to reason critically, and to analyze and solve problems logically." Lexington is committed to promoting a caring environment that fosters a love of learning among its students and an atmosphere of mutual respect and trust. Lexington uses the communication arts as both medium and theme for learning basic skills, exploring the disciplines, and having students demonstrate what they know. Students keep journals, publish newspapers, booklets, and other printed material, and use cinema and other visual material as ways to organize, study, and present the curriculum. Sixth-graders, for example, integrated the curriculum recently by studying environmental issues along the Mason River and then preparing an hour-long documentary film themed to "River Life Today and Tomorrow." Lexington is committed to providing students with a variety of creative opportunities to enhance the learning process. Our observations are summarized next:

Teaching and Learning

- The students at Lexington Learning Academy are enthusiastic, motivated, and deeply involved in the learning process.

- Students, parents, and teachers take pride in their school.

- The wide use of activities that involve students in learning accompanied by positive feedback promotes student self-esteem.

- A variety of age-appropriate student work is assigned and displayed in the classrooms and hallways of the school.

- Lexington teachers are knowledgeable in their subject matter, sensitive to the developmental needs of their students, and committed to their success.

- The learning environment at Lexington is friendly, caring, and supportive.

- Cultural diversity was found to be a high priority and was evidenced by classroom activities, student projects, and corroborated by interviews.

- Teachers and students expressed concern about lack of space in the school.

- Some classes are held in the hallways and in other non-classroom areas.

- The students ate lunch in their classrooms. Many teachers and students expressed a desire for a cafeteria. A vocal minority, however, felt that the present situation helped build a tighter sense of community within the classroom.

- Large class size is a concern. The staff seems aware of the research linking small class size to student performance, and this adds to the concern.

- Classroom management was found to be inconsistent at some grade levels, and this affected student time on task.

Learning Processes

- Many teacher-directed lessons were observed. Hands-on activities were observed primarily in science and social studies classes.

- Frequent field trips provided enrichment of the curriculum and enhanced opportunities for authentic learning.

- Positive study habits and skills were developed through the use of a homework hotline and a neighborhood homeroom center set up in two different apartment complexes.

- The use of higher-order thinking skills was observed in some classrooms but not others.

Instructional Strategies

- Real-life situations were emphasized through interesting and meaningful activities.

- Provisions for building upon prior learning were observed in most classrooms.

- The communication arts theme was not used as consistently as teachers had hoped.

- The Saxon math curriculum provides opportunities for hands-on and higher-level thinking, but there are inconsistencies in its use. Some teachers reported they disliked this system, claiming it "scripts" what they teach and how they are to teach it.

- The school combines a phonics-based and literature-based approach to reading. Students enjoy reading and were heard discussing the stories they read.

- Teachers were enthusiastic about "writing across the curriculum." This approach supported the integration of subjects and promoted the development of skills within a variety of learning contexts.

Student Responses

- Students appear enthusiastic in giving responses.

- Students consistently contribute to one another's learning and share their work with each other.

- Students were frequently observed helping and encouraging their peers.

- The mentoring program provides a positive model for student learning.

- Students seem to want to learn, cooperate with their teachers, and seem willing to take responsibility.

Questions for Reflection

- In what ways can existing space be more efficiently used to accommodate the demands of existing programs?

- How can the school expand its use of technology as an integral part of the curriculum and place emphasis on technology as a tool for learning and productivity?

- How does the emphasis on direct instruction in most curriculum areas distract from or complement the more experiential methods of teaching found at the margins of the curriculum?

- Is classroom management of sufficient concern to warrant further self-study by the Lexington faculty?

- How can the school increase opportunities for students to use critical thinking skills across all grade levels and across the curriculum?

- Would the communication arts theme be more prominent if teachers worked together to develop teaching units and if teaching units were cataloged by grade level and made available to all teachers?

Even though this excerpt is fictional, it is based on actual school reports and thus gives a fuller idea of what might be covered in an external review report. This excerpt focuses only on teaching and learning. An outline of the topics that would be discussed in a complete report is provided in Chapter Six.

Appendix B

Excerpts from an External Review

Following are excerpts from an external review of an elementary school in New York State. The sections presented are (1) teaching and professional development and (2) curriculum and assessment.

Reflections on Teaching and Professional Development

(Practices Observed; Teaching) It was immediately clear to the review team that Highland teachers are totally invested in their teaching. You care about what and how your students learn. You want them to be successful. All staff members exhibit deep commitment to students, extending well beyond the contractual school day. As part of this commitment, staff take on a variety of roles—teacher, mentor, and facilitator of learning. We observed teachers engaging in many curricular and extracurricular activities that are student centered. These included many activities in which staff served as facilitators of learning rather than solely as transmitters of information. We also observed staff working with students on a variety of traditional extracurricular activities such as fund raisers, aerobics classes, and stamp club. Activities such as the post office, the school store, the 5th grade camp-out, the archaeology dig, Energy,

---

Source: Ancess, 1996, pp. 109–114.

Inc., and recycling provided teachers with opportunities to facilitate active learning experiences for students where their engagement can be deepened.

Cooperative Learning Strategies

Some teachers are implementing cooperative learning strategies in their classrooms. These activities actively engaged students with one another and with their tasks.

- During a reading extension activity, students were working in cooperative groups to compare and contrast living in Tonawanda to living in San Francisco.

- During a language arts lesson, student groups were creating a poster based on antonyms.

- In a reading lesson, students cooperatively created a set of directions for carrying out an everyday activity such as making a peanut butter and jelly sandwich.

- In Grade 6 Science, students were researching hot air balloons. They designed their own covers for their projects, which they shared with one another. Students then worked in cooperative groups to make miniature hot air balloons out of tissue paper. Instructions were left on the overhead projector as students read each step and together constructed their balloons.

Interdisciplinary Instruction

Other teachers are beginning to move toward interdisciplinary activities.

- Teachers of 6th grade, which is semi-departmentalized, are beginning to work together to create interdisciplinary units. Two teachers at this grade level arranged a half-day of released time to plan a unit that culminates in a balloon launch and competition. Also in the 6th grade, a teacher developed a spelling list that incorporates vocabulary words from other subject areas.

- At another grade level, a teacher explained to students how the story they were reading about a child who had moved into a new neighborhood linked with the social studies unit on immigrants.

- In a music lesson, student groups chose a poem and selected musical instruments that they then played to make the sounds of the key words.

- In the area of educational technology, students in a few classrooms are using the computer word processing program to produce original writing. Graphics are being integrated into the final products.

There is additional abundant evidence of good teaching practice. Examples include:

Responsive Teaching Strategies

Teaching strategies that are responsive to students' needs, interests, and activities extend opportunities for deepened learning and understanding.

- In a Grade 4 current events lesson, the teacher's active and responsive listening to students' responses prompted questions that further extended opportunities for students to share their reactions to the current events and one another. The teacher asked: "Why do you suppose that's so?" "What could we do to help them?"

- In a Grade 5 mathematics lesson, many students had the opportunity to provide answers. Students shared their conceptual understanding of decimals and responded to each other's concepts.

- In a Grade 5 resource room lesson, two students kept reading logs about a book they were reading. They predicted what might happen next in the story. They took turns reading paragraphs orally and were encouraged to risk decoding and pronouncing unfamiliar words. As students were encouraged to risk in a safe environment, they analyzed their errors and took responsibility for correcting them: "I was right." "I'm forgetting that 'I'. . . ." were student responses. These students recognized and were proud of their own development—they knew how they had made progress.

- In a Grade 5 reading lesson, the teacher began the lesson with what the students knew and built on it in a manner that was meaningful to students. The students shared personal experiences directly related to the topic. Students posed questions that led to discussion.

- In a Grade 5 reading/language arts lesson, a teacher modelled how to write a limerick. The teacher began by reading a limerick written on the board. The students then chanted the limerick and clapped the rhythm.

Students commented to the review team that they learn best when teachers use strategies such as modelling, when they provide multiple examples to clarify the steps in a task as well as the outcomes expected, and when students have opportunities to clarify the tasks they must do, when they have choices, [and] when their interests and varied abilities are challenged and incorporated into the instruction provided.

Learner-Centered Teaching Strategies

As the previous examples attest, teacher-directed instruction is highly evolved at Highland. Occasions where instruction was student centered provided evidence of students taking responsibility for their learning. The resource room reading lesson is one example. Another example was provided by a teacher as he described how he helps his students to plan and conduct the conferences that he holds with their parents. Another is the Hometown USA project.

The review team would like to recommend that teachers expand their teaching repertoire to develop a variety of learner-centered teaching strategies that provide students with increased opportunities for individual and collaborative activities and projects, that require students to use creativity, problem solving, and critical thinking skills, that challenge their range of abilities and interests, and that endure over longer periods of time (e.g., a week, two weeks, or a month). Such projects might require students to apply skills and knowledge learned in reading and mathematics as well as engage in problem solving.

(Professional Development; Opportunities for Professional Development) Teachers are actively engaged in professional development, which we define broadly as participation in activities and events that advance the work of the school. Some of these are teacher initiated, such as the Teacher to Teacher meetings and the use of a teacher consultant who helped staff integrate higher level thinking skills into classroom instruction. Others are district or building initiated, such as the Building Leadership Team and the Education Support Team. An example of a specific professional development activity that the review team finds significant is the school staff's collaborative development of a set of belief statements about the school.

However, much of the professional development available to school staff is district determined. While many Highland staff participate in these activities, they may not meet the professional development needs that would actually be identified by Highland staff.

For example, a need for 6th grade common planning time to develop a common thematic unit has been identified. Common planning for other professional development initiatives would be useful. The team suggests that Highland consider renegotiating the use of the eight half-days currently used for parent conferences so that a portion are used for professional development. Perhaps the faculty might evaluate this change at the end of one year and regularly assess the use of these days as they impact on student achievement and outcomes. Additionally, planning time might be organized for the work.

Redefining Teacher Roles

The review team identified the use of teaching resources as a concern among staff. We recommend an assessment of teacher roles, especially in how special teachers are utilized. The BLT might want to assess the degree to which the talents and skills of these teachers are being effectively utilized from their perspective, from the perspective of the classroom teachers, [and] from the perspective of student growth and achievement. The BLT might want to consider alternative roles to the ones currently in place for special teachers to determine which are most effective in terms of student learning. Examples might be the consultant model as opposed to the pull-out model, or team teaching, or joint planning between special teachers and classroom teachers.

Questions for Consideration

Given the degree to which teaching practice appears to be teacher centered, the review team would like to pose these questions to Highland staff for consideration:

- What steps will Highland take to develop an explicit and consistent pedagogical philosophy that continues to build on your belief statements (e.g., "The purpose of Highland School is to develop each student's ability to think and reason")?

- How can you both seek new learner-centered teaching strategies and recognize and use the expertise currently residing in staff members?

Reflections on Curriculum and Assessment

(Practices Observed; Curriculum):

- The staff of the Highland School is rightfully proud of the richness of their curricular offerings. A wide variety of learning opportunities are provided to students in heterogeneously grouped classes during the regular and extended school day. These opportunities reflect a range of multidisciplinary projects, such as the Civil War bike trip; the archeological dig; the poems, stories, and art work comprising the student anthology; and the Thanksgiving dinner served by costumed 4th grade students to their parents.

- The staff cooperatively prepared a school logo that reflects the theme of learning, respect, and responsibility identified in the School Improvement Plan.

- The school environment and curriculum give evidence of the concern for promoting respect among students and faculty for each other. Respect for members of the larger, global community was fostered through curriculum such as music from a variety of world cultures. In a 6th grade reading class, a story depicting a multicultural perspective was discussed in the context of a talk given by an African American at the school last year.

- Teachers have developed curriculum that actively engages students. Examples include: a 5th grade class that was cooperatively engaged in testing and recording the properties of minerals; a 6th grade class set up as a micro-society, where students made decisions about finances, business, and social issues; and 4th grade classes in which students dressed as the historical characters they researched for projects on Famous Americans.

- Interdisciplinary curriculum was evident in art where students used science books as a resource for drawing underwater life. Fifth graders connected the novel they were reading on a family leaving a small town to their social studies immigration unit. Sixth grade students integrated skills from various disciplines in their Hometown USA project.

- Curricular activities such as visiting authors, pride days, and book fairs are examples of the use of curriculum to achieve the school goals of improvement of reading and increased motivation in reading.

Questions for Consideration

- How can Highland expand students' opportunities to develop respect and to value the contributions of diverse cultures? • How can Highland use diversity as a context to further enhance curricular content? • In order to promote the intellectual development of students, how might Highland develop more long term, hands on, problem-solving activities that integrate learning in mathematics, science, language, social studies, and the arts as opposed to short, individual lessons in isolated content areas?

Assessments

(Multiple Forms of Student Assessment)

- Highland celebrates student achievement in a variety of ways including the House of Honor [and] award assemblies both of which recognize students who demonstrate quality learning.

- Teachers use charts, stickers, and awards as means of motivating increased student achievement.

- Highland faculty have indicated an interest in authentic assessment. Authentic assessment practices included: opportunities for sixth grade students to demonstrate their understanding by serving as guides to the archeological digs for the fourth graders; opportunities for self and peer assessment in preparation for teacher conferences with their own parents and through classroom critiques of each other's work; opportunities for students in instrumental and choral music programs to assess and analyze their own performances. In two cases, students generated and displayed assessment criteria for quality learning and teaching.

Program Assessment

- The faculty has compiled standardized test results for use in assessing the outcomes of the instructional program.

Questions for Consideration

- To what degree do standardized tests drive curriculum and instructional strategies? • How will Highland use multiple sources of information to assess children's progress? • How will Highland assess the effectiveness and appropriateness of diverse teaching strategies to achieve the student outcomes stated in the school's and district's goals? • How will Highland assess the effectiveness and appropriateness of curriculum to achieve the student outcomes stated in the school's and district's goals?

Endnotes

1. I rely heavily on Jürgen Habermas's ideas as presented in his book *The Theory of Communicative Action*, Vol. 2. *Lifeworld and System: A Critique of Functional Reason*. This book was translated into English by Thomas McCarthy in 1987 and published by the Beacon Press in Boston. Habermas uses the language "systems" and "lifeworlds" to describe two mutually exclusive yet ideally interdependent domains of all of society's enterprises from the family to the complex formal organization. Habermas's theory is influenced by the works of Mead, Parsons, and many others. I take some liberties with the technicalities of his discussion in order to use his overarching theory as a framework for understanding the cultural world of schools and how this world can be compromised. A compromised cultural world can have serious negative developmental and academic effects for children. I use his overarching theory, as well, to show what we need to do to protect ourselves from these effects. See also Gayle Spry and Bill Sultman (1994), *Journeying in Renewal: A Resource for Self-renewing Catholic Schools*. This book, published by the Catholic Department of Education, Archdiocese of Brisbane, provides a lively discussion of Habermas's theory applied to school renewal.

2. The discussion of community in this chapter is based on "Moral Authority, Community and Diversity: Leadership Challenges for the 21st Century" address, Center for Educational Leadership, University of Hong Kong, December 4, 1998, and "The Elementary School as Community in a Diverse Society," McMillan Lecture, Grosse Pointe Academy, March 10, 1999.

3. This discussion of change strategies, the reason for their selection, and their effects on schools is based on "Organization, Market and Community as Strategies for Change: What Works Best for Deep Changes in Schools?" by T. J. Sergiovanni. In A. Hargreaves, A. Lieberman, M. Fullan, and D. Hopkins (eds.), *International Handbook of Educational Change*, Part I. Boston: Kluwer Academic Publishers, 1998, pp. 571–596.

References

Ancess, J. *Outside/Inside, Inside/Outside: Developing and Implementing the School Quality Review*. New York: National Center for Restructuring Education, Schools and Teaching, 1996.

Anderson, H., Boyle, C. S., Lopez, N., and Moore, L. B. "Ripples that Touch the Future." International School of the Americas, San Antonio, Texas, Dec. 1997.

Argyris, C. *Integrating the Individual and the Organization*. New York: Wiley, 1964.

Argyris, C. *Organization and Innovation*. Homewood, Ill.: Irwin, 1965.

Argyris, C. *Intervention Theory and Method: A Behavioral Science View*. Reading, Mass.: Addison-Wesley, 1970.

Arrowsmith, W. A. "The Calling of Teaching." In D. E. Purpel and H. S. Shapiro (eds.), *Schools and Meaning Essays on the Moral Nature of Schooling*. Lanham, Md.: University Press of America, 1985.

Ashton, P. J., and Webb, R. B. *Making a Difference: Teachers' Sense of Efficacy and Student Achievement*. New York: Longman, 1986.

Bandura, A. "Self-efficacy: Toward a Unifying Theory of Behavioral Change." *Psychological Review*, 1977, *84*, 191–215.

Bandura, A. "Self-efficacy: Mechanisms in Human Agency." *American Psychologist*, 1982, *87*(2), 122–147.

Battistich, V., Solomon, D., Watson, M., and Schaps, E. "Students and Teachers in Caring Communities and School Communities." Paper presented at the annual meeting of the American Educational Research Association, New Orleans, Apr. 1994.

Beck, L. *Reclaiming Educational Administration as a Caring Profession*. New York: Teachers College Press, 1994.

Bellah, R. N., and others. *Habits of the Heart: Individualism and Commitment in American Life*. New York: HarperCollins, 1985.

Benne, K. D. "Democratic Ethics and Social Engineering." *Progressive Education*, 1949, *27*(7).

Bieser, K., and Baize, J. "School Culture: A Study in Contrasts." Department of Education, Trinity University, Apr. 1998.

Bimber, B. "School Decentralization Lessons from the Study of Bureaucracy." Institute of Education and Training. Santa Monica, Calif.: RAND Corporation, 1993.

Blau, P. M., and Scott, W. R. *Formal Organizations: A Comparative Approach*. San Francisco: Chandler, 1962.

Blomqvist, C. Interview Transcript, "International School of the Americas: San Antonio, Texas." July 3, 1998.

Botstein, L. "Language and Hope." *Education Week*, Nov. 5, 1997, p. 39. Cited in Botstein, L. *Jefferson's Children: Education and the Promise of American Culture*. New York: Doubleday, 1997.

"Breaking Ranks: Changing an American Institution." Report of the National Association of Secondary School Principals on the High School for the 21st Century. Reston, Va.: National Association of Secondary School Principals, 1996.

Bronowski, J. *The Origins of Knowledge and Imagination*. New Haven, Conn.: Yale University Press, 1978.

Broudy, H. S. "Conflict in Values." In R. Ohm and W. Monoham (eds.), *Educational Administration: Philosophy in Action*. Norman: University of Oklahoma, College of Education, 1965.

Bryk, A. S., and Driscoll, M. E. *The School as Community: Theoretical Foundations, Contextual Influences and Consequences for Teachers and Students*. Madison, Wis.: National Center for Effective Secondary Schools, 1988.

Bryk, A. S., Lee, V. L., and Holland, P. B. *Catholic Schools and the Common Good*. Cambridge: Harvard University Press, 1993.

Bryk, A. S., Sebring, P. B., Kerbow, D., Rollow, S., and Easton, J. Q. *Charting School Reform: Democratic Localism as a Lever for Change*. Boulder, Colo.: Westview Press, 1998.

Chubb, J. E., and Moe, T. M. *Politics, Markets, and America's Schools*. Washington, D.C.: Brookings Institution, 1990.

Clinchy, E. "Why are we Restructuring?" *New Schools, New Communities*, Spring 1995, *11*(3), 7–12.

Coleman, J. "Social Capital in the Creation of Human Capital." *American Journal of Sociology*, 1988, *94*, 95–120.

Coleman, J. *Foundations of Social Theory*. Cambridge, Mass.: Harvard University Press, 1990.

Coleman, J., and Hoffer, T. *Public and Private High Schools: The Impact of Communities*. New York: Basic Books, 1987.

Commission on the Reorganization of Secondary Education. *Cardinal Principles of Secondary Education*. Washington, D.C.: Government Printing Office, 1918.

Conger, J. A., and Kanungo, R. N. "Toward a Behavioral Theory of Charismatic Leadership in Organizational Settings." *Academy of Management Review*, 1987, *12*(4), 637–647.

Conger, J. A., and Kanungo, R. N. "Behavioral Dimensions of Charismatic Leadership." In J. A. Conger and R. N. Kanungo (eds.), *Charismatic Leadership*. San Francisco: Jossey-Bass, 1988.

Cuban, L. "A Tale of Two Schools," *Education Week*, Jan. 28, 1998, p. 33.

Cusick, P. A. *The Education System: Its Nature and Logic*. New York: McGraw-Hill, Inc, 1992.

Darling-Hammond, L. "What Matters Most? A Competent Teacher for Every Child." *Phi Beta Kappan*, 1996, *78*(3), 193–200.

Darling-Hammond, L. *The Right to Learn: A Blueprint for Creating Schools That Work*. San Francisco: Jossey-Bass, 1997.

Darling-Hammond, L., and Falk, B. "Using Standards and Assessments to Support Student Learning." *Phi Delta Kappan*, Nov. 1997, *79*, 190–199.

Darwin, C. *The Origin of Species by Means of Natural Selection*. Harmondsworth, N.Y.: Penguin, 1985.

De Charms, R. *Personal Causation*. New York: Academic Press, 1968.

Deiro, J. "Teacher Strategies for Nurturing Healthy Connections with Students." *Journal of a Just and Caring Education*, Apr. 1997, *3*(2), 192–202.

Deiro, J. *Teaching with Heart: Making Connections with Students*. Thousand Oaks, Calif.: Corwin Press, 1996.

Department of Education. *Implementing the Agenda for Change*. Government of Ireland, 1996.

Duttweiler, P. C. "A Broader Definition of Effective Schools: Implications From Research and Practice." In T. J. Sergiovanni and J. H. Moore (eds.), *Target 2000: A Compact for Excellence in Texas's Schools*. Austin: Texas Association for Supervision and Curriculum Development, 1990.

Eisner, E. *The Educational Imagination*. (2nd ed.) New York: Macmillan, 1991.

Elias, M. and others. *Promoting Social and Emotional Learning: Guidelines for Educators*. Alexandria, Va.: Association for Supervision and Curriculum Development, 1997.

Elmore, R., Peterson, P., and McCartney, S. *Restructuring in the Classroom: Teaching, Learning, and School Organization*. San Francisco: Jossey-Bass, 1996.

Etzioni, A. *The Moral Dimension: Toward a New Economics*. New York: Free Press, 1988.

Etzioni, A. *The Spirit of Community: Rights, Responsibilities and the Communitarian Agenda*. New York: Crown, 1993.

Etzioni, A. (ed.). *New Communitarian Thinking: Persons, Virtues, Institutions and Communities*. Charlottesville, Va.: University of Virginia Press, 1995.

Etzioni, A. *The New Golden Rule: Community and Morality in a Democratic Society*. New York: Basic Books, 1996.

Etzioni, A. "The Community of Communities." *The Responsive Community Rights and Responsibilities*, Winter 1996/97, 7(1), 21–32.

Fukuyama, F. *Trust: The Social Virtues and the Creation of Prosperity*. London: Hamish Hamilton, 1995.

Fullan, M. *The New Meaning of Educational Change*. (2nd ed.) New York: Teachers College Press, 1991.

Fullan, M. *Change Forces*. New York: Falmer Press, 1993.

Fullinwider, R. K. "Civic Education and Traditional Values." *Philosophy and Public Policy*, 1986, 6(3).

Furman, G. C. "Postmodernism and Community in Schools: Unravelling the Paradox." *Educational Administration Quarterly*, 1998, 34(3), 298–328.

Gamoran, A. "Student Achievement in Public Magnet, Public Comprehensive and Private City High Schools." *Educational Evaluation and Policy Analysis*, 1996, 18(1), 1–18.

Gardner, H. *Dreams of Mind: The Theory of Multiple Intelligences*. New York: Basic Books, 1983.

Gardner, H. *The Multiple Intelligences: The Theory in Practice*. New York: Basic Books, 1993.

Gardner, H. *Leading Minds: An Anatomy of Leadership*. New York: Basic Books, 1995.

Goleman, D. *Emotional Intelligence*. New York: Bantam, 1995.

Goodlad, J. *A Place Called School*. New York: McGraw-Hill, 1983.

Grant, G. P. *The World We Created at Hamilton High*. Cambridge: Harvard University Press, 1988.

Green, D. "Crafting a System: Accountability and Quality Assurance in Illinois Schools." New York: Institute for Education and Social Policy, New York University, 1995.

Greenfield, T. B. "Organizations as Social Inventions: Rethinking Assumptions about Change." *Journal of Applied Behavioral Science*, 1973, 9(5).

Greenfield, T. B. "Leaders and Schools: Willfulness and Non-natural Order in Organizations." In T. J. Sergiovanni and J. E. Corbally (eds.), *Leadership and Organizational Culture*. Urbana-Champaign: University of Illinois Press, 1984.

Grob, L. "Leadership: The Socratic Model." In B. Kellerman (ed.), *Leadership: Multidisciplinary Perspectives*. Englewood Cliffs, N.J.: Prentice Hall, 1984.

Habermas, J. *The Theory of Communicative Action*. Vol. 2: *Lifeworld and System: A Critique of Functional Reason*. (T. McCarthy, trans.) Boston: Beacon Press, 1987.

Hebert, E. A. "Portfolios Invite Reflection—From Students and Staff." *Educational Leadership*, May 1992, 49(8), 58–61.

Heyward, C. *Touching our Strength: The Erotic and the Love of God*. San Francisco: Harper & Row, 1989.

Hill, P. T., Foster, G. E., and Gendler, T. *High Schools with Character*, R3944-RC. Santa Monica, Calif.: RAND Corporation, 1990.

Hoff, D. J. "Panel Assails Assessment Calculations." *Education Week*, Sept. 30, 1998a, p. 23.

Hoff, D. J. "At Long Last, California Board Adopts Standards for All Core Disciplines." *Education Week*, Oct. 21, 1998b, p. 12.

Hollenbach, D. "Virtue, the Common Good, and Democracy." In A. Etzioni (ed.), *New Communitarian Thinking*. Charlottesville, Va.: University of Virginia Press, 1995.

Huberman, M. "Teacher Professionalism and Workplace Conditions." A memorandum for the Holmes Group Seminar: Conceptions of Teachers' Work and the Organization of Schools, Sept. 1988.

Hunter, J. D. *Before the Shooting Begins: Searching for Democracy in America's Cultural War*. New York: Free Press, 1994.

Illinois State Board of Education. *Accountability and Quality Assurance Guidelines: 1997–98*, Draft II. Springfield: Center for Accountability and Quality Assurance, 1997–1998.

Illinois State Board of Education. *Internal Review Manual*. Springfield: Division of Quality Assurance and Improvement Planning, Feb. 1998.

International School of the Americas. "The ISA Senior Portfolio and Exhibition." North East Independent School District, San Antonio, Texas, 1998.

Johnson, S. M. *Leading to Change*. San Francisco: Jossey-Bass, 1996.

Johnston, R. C. "California Poll Finds Support for State Action on Schools." *Education Week*, Mar. 11, 1998.

Jones, C. Personal communication, May 1997.

Kao, J. *Jamming: The Art and Discipline of Business Creativity*. London: Harper-Collins, 1996.

Kaplan, R. D. "Was Democracy Just a Moment?" *Atlantic Monthly*, Dec. 1997, p. 15.

Kegan, R., and Lahey, L. L. "Adult Leadership and Adult Development: A Constructionist View." In B. Kellerman (ed.), *Leadership: Multidisciplinary Perspectives*. Englewood Cliffs, N.J.: Prentice Hall, 1984.

Kennedy, M. M. "Inexact Sciences: Professional Education and the Development of Expertise." East Lansing, Mich.: The National Center for Research on Teacher Education, 1987.

Kernan-Schloss, A., and Plattner, A. "Talking to the Public about Public Schools." *Educational Leadership*, 1998, 56(2), 18–22.

Klonsky, M. *Small Schools: The Numbers Tell a Story*. Chicago: The Small Schools Workshop, University of Illinois at Chicago, 1996.

Lambert, L. "How to Build Leadership Capacity." *Educational Leadership*, 1998, 55(7), 17–19.

Lambert, L., and others. *The Constructivist Leader*. New York: Teachers College Press, 1995.

Lightfoot, S. L. *The Good High School: Portraits of Character and Culture*. New York: Basic Books, 1983.

Lipsitz, J. *Successful Schools for Young Adolescents*. New Brunswick, N.J.: Transaction Books, 1984.

Louis, M. R. "Surprise and Sense-making: What Newcomers Experience in Entering Unfamiliar Organizational Settings." *Administrator Science Quarterly*, 1980, 25, 226–251.

MacBeath, J. *Talking about Schools*. Edinburgh: Scottish Education Department, Her Majesty's School Office, 1989.

MacBeath, J., Boyd, B., Rand, J., and Bell, S. *Schools Speak for Themselves: Toward a Framework for Self-evaluation*. London: The National Union of Teachers, 1995.

Mac Cormack, J. "Schools' Closure Tears Tiny Town." *San Antonio Express News*, Sept. 7, 1998, p. 4A.

Mannheim, K. *Man and Society in an Age of Reconstruction*. New York: Harcourt Brace, 1940.

March, J. G., and Simon, H. A. *Organizations*. New York: Wiley, 1958.

Marks, H., and Louis, K. S. "Does Teacher Empowerment Affect the Classroom? The Implications of Teacher Empowerment for Teachers' Instructional Practice and Student Academic Performance." *Educational Evaluation and Policy Analysis*, Vol. 14, no. 3, 1997, pp. 245–275.

Marzano, R. J., and Kendall, J. S. *Designing Standards-Based Districts, Schools and Classrooms.* Aurora, Colo.: McREL, 1996.

Mayeroff, M. *On Caring.* New York: Harper & Row, 1971.

McGaw, B., and others. *Improving Schools through Public Consultation: The Australian Effective Schools Project.* Victoria, British Columbia: ICSEI, 1992.

Meier, D. *The Power of Their Ideas: Lessons for America From a Small School in Harlem.* Boston: Beacon Press, 1995.

Mintzberg, H. *The Structure of Organizations.* New York: Wiley, 1979.

Mintzberg, H. "Crafting Strategy." *Harvard Business Review,* July-Aug. 1987, 66–75.

Moe, T. "The New Economics of Organizations." *American Journal of Political Science,* 1984, 28(4), 739–777.

National Association of Secondary School Principals. *Breaking Ranks: Changing an American Institution.* Report, Mar. 1996.

National Commission on Excellence in Education. *A Nation at Risk: The Full Account.* USA Research, Inc., 1983.

National Commission on Teaching and America's Future. *What Matters Most: Teaching for America's Future.* New York: The Commission, 1996.

National Conference of Catholic Bishops. *To Teach as Jesus Did: A Pastoral Message on Catholic Education.* Washington, D.C.: U.S. Catholic Conference, 1973.

Newmann, F. M., Marks, H., and Gamoran, A. "Authentic Pedagogy: Standards that Boost Student Performance." Issues in Restructuring School." Report No. 8, Spring. Madison: Center on Organization and Restructuring of Schools, University of Wisconsin, 1995.

Newmann, F. M., Secada, W. G., and Wehlage, G. G. *A Guide to Authentic Instrumentation and Assessment: Vision, Standards and Scoring.* Madison: Wisconsin Center for Education Research, 1995.

Nias, J. "Teachers' Moral Purposes: Sources of Vulnerability and Strength." The Johann Jacobs Foundation Conference on Teacher Burnout, Marbach Castle, Germany, Nov. 1995.

Nias, J., Southworth, G., and Yeomans, R. *Staff Relationships in the Primary School: A Study of Organizational Cultures.* London: Cassell, 1989.

Noddings, N. *The Challenge to Care in Schools: An Alternative Approach to Education.* New York: Teachers College Press, 1992.

Nothwehr, D. "A Lesson from a Sarcastic Jesus." *Catholic Education: A Journal of Inquiry and Practice,* 1998a, 2(2), 82–97.

Nothwehr, D. *Mutuality: A Formal Norm for Christian Social Ethics.* San Francisco: Catholic Scholars Press, 1998b.

Olson, S. "Science Friction." *Education Week*, Sept. 30, 1998, 25–29.

Ouchi, W. G. "Markets, Bureaucracies and Clans." *Administrative Science Quarterly*, 1980, 25(1), 129–141.

Palmer, P. J. "Evoking the Spirit in Public Education." *Educational Leadership*, 1998, 56(4), 6–11.

Peters, T. J., and Waterman, R. H. *In Search of Excellence: Lessons from America's Best Run Companies*. New York: Harper & Row, 1982.

Pew Forum on Educational Reform. "Strategies for Fixing Failing Public Schools." *Education Week*, Nov. 4, 1998, 42–47.

Pierce v. Society of Sisters, 268 U.S. 510, 1925.

Plato. *Theaetetus*, in *Plato's Theory of Knowledge: The Theaetetus and the Sophist of Plato*. (F. M. Cornford, Trans.) New York: Bobbs, Merrill, 1957.

Quartz, K. H. "Sustaining New Educational Communities Toward a New Culture of School Reform." In J. Oakes and K. H. Quartz (eds.), *Creating New Educational Communities*. Ninety fourth Yearbook of the National Society for the Study of Education, Part I. Chicago: University of Chicago Press, 1995.

Quinn, J. B. "Formulating Strategy One Step at a Time." *Journal of Business Strategy*, 1981, 1(3).

Sacks, J. "Rebuilding Civil Society: A Biblical Perspective." *Responsive Community*, 1997, 7(1), 11–20.

"San Antonio International School of the Americas, Living and Learning in Today's Global Market Place: A Prospectus." Center for Educational Leadership, Trinity University, San Antonio, Texas, 1993.

Savill, R. "Love-Triangle Teacher 'Dreading New Term'." *Daily Telegraph*, Jan. 6, 1998, p. 3.

Schön, D. *The Reflective Practitioner: How Professionals Think in Action*. New York: Basic Books, 1983.

Schultz, T. W. "Human Capital Approaches in Organizing and Paying for Education." In W. McMahan and T. G. Geste (eds.), *Financing Education: Overcoming Inefficiency and Inequity*. Urbana-Champaign: University of Illinois Press, 1982.

Schwartz, B. *The Costs of Living: How Market Freedom Erodes the Best Things in Life*. New York: Norton, 1994.

Sebring, P. B., and Bryk, A. S. "Student Centered Learning Climate." In Sebring and others, *Charting Reform in Chicago: The Students Speak*. A report sponsored by the Consortium on Chicago School Research. Chicago: University of Chicago, 1996.

Selznick, P. *Leadership in Administration*. Berkeley: University of California Press, 1957.

Sergiovanni, T. J. *Value-Added Leadership*. San Diego: Harcourt, Harcourt Brace, 1990.

Sergiovanni, T. J. *Moral Leadership: Getting to the Heart of School Improvement*. San Francisco: Jossey-Bass, 1992.

Sergiovanni, T. J. *Building Community in Schools*. San Francisco: Jossey-Bass, 1994.

Sergiovanni, T. J. *The Principalship: A Reflective Practice Perspective*. (3rd ed.) Boston: Allyn & Bacon, 1995.

Sergiovanni, T. J. *Leadership for the Schoolhouse: How Is It Different? Why Is It Important?* San Francisco: Jossey-Bass, 1996.

Sergiovanni, T. J. "Moral Authority, Community and Diversity: Leadership Challenges for the 21st Century." Inauguration Conference, Centre for Educational Leadership, University of Hong Kong, Dec. 1998.

Sergiovanni, T. J. "Organization, Market and Community as Strategies for Change: What Works Best for Deep Changes in Schools?" In A. Hargreaves, A. Lieberman, M. Fullan, and D. Hopkins (eds.), *International Handbook of Educational Change*, Part I. Boston: Kluwer Academic Publishers, 1998.

Sergiovanni, T. J. "The Elementary School as Community in a Diverse Society." William Charles McMillan III Lecture, Grosse Pointe Academy, Grosse Point Farms, Mich., Mar. 10, 1999. ©T.J.S.

Sergiovanni, T. J., and Elliott, D. *Educational and Organizational Leadership in Elementary Schools*. Englewood Cliffs, N.J.: Prentice Hall, 1975.

Sergiovanni, T. J., and Starratt, R. J. *Supervision: A Redefinition*. (6th ed.) New York: McGraw-Hill, 1998.

Sergiovanni, T. J. *Rethinking Leadership*. Arlington Heights, Ill.: SkyLight Training and Publishing, 1999.

Shouse, R. C. "Academic Press and a Sense of Community: Conflict, Congruence, and Implications for Student Achievement." *Social Psychology of Education*, 1996, *1*, 47–68.

Skinner, B. F. *Science and Human Behavior*. New York: Macmillan, 1953.

Smith, A. *An Inquiry into the Nature and Causes of the Wealth of Nations*. New York: Modern Library, 1937. (Originally published 1776.)

Sowell, T. *A Conflict of Visions*. New York: Morrow, 1987.

Spady, W. "Educentric Testing Undermines America's Future." *Education Week*, Oct. 7, 1998, pp. 36, 38.

Spry, G., and Sultman, B. *Journeying in Renewal: A Resource for Self-renewing Catholic Schools*. Brisbane: Brisbane Catholic Education, 1994.

Starratt, R. J. *Transforming Educational Administration: Meaning, Community and Excellence*. New York: McGraw-Hill, 1996.

Staw, B. "Leadership and Persistence." In T. J. Sergiovanni and J. E. Corbally (eds.), *Leadership and Organizational Culture*. Urbana-Champaign: University of Illinois Press, 1984.

Steinberg, L., Brown, B., and Dornbusch, S. M. *Beyond the Classroom: Why School Reform has Failed and What Parents Need to Do*. New York: Simon & Schuster, 1996.

Sternberg, R. J., and Wagner, R. (eds.). *Practical Intelligence*. New York: Cambridge University Press, 1995.

Sternberg, R. J. "What is Successful Intelligence?" *Education Week*, Nov. 13, 1996, p. 48.

Stewart, T. A. *Intellectual Capital*. New York: Doubleday, 1997.

Stinson, R. "Important Discovery Made in Candelaria." *San Antonio Express News*, Sept. 7, 1995, p. 3A.

Sunstein, C. R. "The Enduring Legacy of Republicanism." In S. E. Elkin and K. E. Soltin (eds.), *A New Constitutionalism: Designing Political Institutions for a Good Society*. Chicago: University of Chicago Press, 1993.

Suryaraman, M. "School District Achieves Lots with Little: Resourceful and Focused, Evergreen Shines Despite 'Difficult' Demographics." *San Jose Mercury News*, Jan. 30, 1997.

Taylor, C. "Liberal Politics and the Public Sphere." In A. Etzioni (ed.), *New Communitarian Thinking: Persons, Virtue, Institutions and Communities*. Charlottesville, Va.: University of Virginia Press, 1995.

Tucker, M. S., and Codding, J. B. *Standards for Our Schools: How to Set Them, Measure Them and Reach Them*. San Francisco: Jossey-Bass, 1997.

van Manen, M. *The Tact of Teaching: The Meaning of Pedagogical Thoughtfulness*. Albany: State University of New York Press, 1991.

Walton, M. *The Deming Management Method*. New York: Putnam Publishing Group, 1986.

Weissberg, R. P., Jackson, A. S., and Shriver, T. P. "Promoting Positive Social Development and Health Practices in Young Urban Adolescents." In M. J. Elias (ed.), *Social Decision Making and Life Skills Development: Guidelines for Middle School Educators*. Gaithersburg, Md.: Aspen, 1993.

West-Burnham, J. "Leadership for Learning—reengineering 'mindsets'." *School Leadership and Management*, 1997, *17*(2), 231–244.

Whitehead, A. N. *Symbolism, Its Meaning and Effect*. New York: Capricorn Books, 1927.

Wiggins, G. *Assessing Student Performance: Exploring the Purpose and Limits of Testing*. San Francisco: Jossey-Bass, 1993.

Wiggins, G. "Practicing What we Preach in Designing Authentic Assessments." *Educational Leadership*, Dec. 1996, *54*(4), 18–25.

William Charles McMillan III Lecture, Grosse Pointe Academy, Grosse Pointe Farms, Michigan, March 10, 1999.

Wills, G. "What Makes a Good Leader?" *The Atlantic Monthly*, Apr. 1994.

Wilson, S. W., and Peterson, P. L. "Theories of Learning and Teaching: What do they Mean for Educators?" Working paper, Benchmarks for Schools. Washington, D.C.: U.S. Department of Education, Office of Educational Research and Improvement, 1997.

Wolk, R. A. "Education's High Stakes Gamble." *Education Week*, Dec. 9, 1998.

Zaleznik, A. *The Managerial Mystique: Restoring Leadership in Business*. New York: Harper & Row, 1989.

Index